Thought: The Invisible Essence

Also by Maurice Whelan and published by Ginninderra Press
Boat People
The Lilac Bow
Excalibur's Return
A Season and a Time
Spirit Eyes

Maurice Whelan

Thought:
The Invisible Essence

Acknowledgements

I am grateful to various people who individually or in a group read and commented upon all or parts of this book as it progressed from draft to completion.

My thanks to Michael Dudley, Dilys Daws, Michelle Epstein, Philip Hewitt, Michael Hannon, Winton Higgins, Catherine Hickie, Tom Ilbery, Elaine Kelly, Richard O'Neill-Dean, Helen Taylor-Robinson, Lorraine Rose, Nick Walker.

I thank the Sydney Institute for Psychoanalysis for hosting the lecture series upon which the book was based and everyone who attended those lectures and whose questions and comments enlarged my understanding.

My continuing thanks to Stephen Matthews for publishing my work.

Dedicated to Neville Symington

Thought: The Invisible Essence
ISBN 978 1 76109 347 0
Copyright © text Maurice Whelan 2022
Cover image: Shahid Najeeb

First published 2022 by
GINNINDERRA PRESS
PO Box 3461 Port Adelaide 5015
www.ginninderrapress.com.au

Contents

Part One — 7
1. From Here to Dublin — 9
2. The Rough Magic of Words — 19
3. An Education in Thinking — 35
4. Blessed Are Those Who Hunger and Thirst After Justice — 47
5. Suffer Little Children to Come to Me — 63
6. Blinded by the Light — 74
7. Introibo Ad Altare Dei — 86
8. Out of the Valley of Darkness — 94

Part Two — 109
9. Introduction — 111
10. On Going On a Journey with William Hazlitt — 114
11. The Best Lived Quietly – Meeting John McGahern — 135
12. To Infinity; and Beyond — 144
13. Living the Dream — 162
14. Summoned by the Tides – Emily Dickinson — 172

Part Three — 181
15. Introduction — 183
16. Too Bright a Light Blinds — 188
17. The Mind as Navigator — 196
18. Old Ground — 202
19. Where Silence Reigns — 204
20. Here is Where I Start From — 209
21. Building Blocks — 214
22. Listening and Learning — 219
23. Good Manners of the Mind — 222

24 Feathers on the Breath of God	229
25 Hope is the Thing	234
26 Places on Earth	240
Bibliography	246
Index	250

Part One

1

From Here to Dublin

Once upon a time, people looked at the world and thought about its parts, and said it was made of four elements, earth, air, fire and water. They looked again, upwards, at the moon, the planets, the stars. 'Are they made of something else?' they asked. 'Another element?' 'A fifth?' And later still they lowered their eyes. Instead of gazing at the wonders around and beyond, they looked inside and began to ask questions about their own minds. At first, it seemed a simple place. They looked again and found it was not. 'Is it,' one asked, 'a universe to itself?'

Time passed. And someone who saw further than others – his name was Heraclitus – said, 'You cannot discover the limit of mind, even if you travel by every path in order to do so; such is the depth of its meaning.'

*

And now to time present. I practise the 'talking cure'. For the past thirty-five years in my daily work, I have contemplated the thoughts of other people, listened to the movements in their minds, helped them to be inquisitive about themselves, to listen, to learn their limits. To become what I am, a psychoanalyst, I first of all had to become a patient. I had to allow someone to observe the movement of my mind, to help me to be inquisitive, to listen, to find my limits, to look beyond, into possibility.

This is a book about thought. All sorts of thought. But before I go forward, I must briefly go back, to explain the title. In Medieval Latin, the fifth element or essence was called *quinta essentia*. It was considered a very fine substance that permeated all being. *Quinta essentia* has given English that beautiful word quintessence, to mean the purest essence of a thing. I am intrigued by the quintessence of thought and grateful that I can name the book you have in your hand *Thought: The Invisible Essence*.

The notion of a 'fifth element or essence', the sense of something beyond and hard to define, outside the usual categories of thinking, goes far beyond Western philosophy and appears in many forms, in other systems of thought. And nowadays, even some physicists use *quinta essentia* to refer to a type of dark matter that (they suspect) makes up three-quarters of the energy in the universe.

Thought, through these pages, is given a wide definition. It extends beyond the confines of the intellectual and the cerebral. Philosophy is a form of thought. So too art and literature. Spirituality and dreaming are considered forms of thought.

I practise the 'writing cure'. Writing occurs in various forms and fulfils many functions. Writing 'cures' when it leads to self-awareness and self-understanding. For me, there are some things that only come together by writing. 'The only time I know the truth,' Jean Malaquais said, 'is when it reveals itself at the point of my pen.' These and words of the Irish writer John McGahern – 'I write because I need to write. I write to see. Through words I see' – are, dare I say, like secular scripture to my soul.

That I decided to write this book is a bit of an accident. Much of what goes on in the mind never gets on the page. There's no need. Before I tell you what got me started, I'll say something about writing itself. These words you are reading did not begin on a keyboard and screen. Nor on a typewriter. I learned to write with a pencil. In a jotter, with a map of my native Ireland on the front, multiplication and addition tables and units of measurements on the back, I first made my mark. I'm no Luddite, but even now, when I start out, the pencil is between my fingers and my thumb. The pencil is a key that unlocks a door. As it opens, I step back into a childlike wonder of words. That same wonder, that sense of magic is always there, waiting. If when writing, I lose touch with wonder and magic, I lose my way.

Now that I'm back there remembering, I see another, earlier jotter. Instead of lines, the pages are full of squares. It was for maths; when adding, subtracting, multiplying and dividing, numbers had to stay in their place. No veering to left or right. Hopefully.

The squares helped with letters. One letter to one square. A frame to play within. What I remember most was making diagonals. The diagonal began in the bottom left-hand corner, moved across and up to the right-hand corner. This encouraged a flowing script. The little lines that link letters are meant to point in the same direction. A line of diagonals should look like a tilted Venetian blind. So I was told.

From back there to here, I have written countless essays during the various courses of studies I have undertaken during my life, numerous professional articles for journals, book reviews, occasional pieces for newspapers and eight books.

I left Ireland in 1971. In London, some years later when working as a social worker, I co-wrote my first book with a teacher. We addressed the challenges faced by children with special educational needs, and paid attention to the risks of marginalising those children in society. Time and I moved on. I was a psychoanalyst. I edited and was the main contributor to a second book, which was completed after I moved to Sydney in 1992. That one centred on Ella Sharpe, who taught English literature for twenty years before becoming a psychoanalyst. My third book was on the life and thought of the writer William Hazlitt, who spanned the end of the eighteenth and the beginning of the nineteenth centuries. Thereafter, I wrote a novel and four books of poetry.

To write well is hard and long. I have never written full-time but my book on William Hazlitt took five years. And apart from my published novel, I wrote two others, each of which took three years. Neither made the publisher's grade. How writers write varies. While ordinary life, work and leisure carries on, as I write, I at least find it necessary to give over a section of my mind to turmoil. Ideas, images, words, phrases, punctuations marks jostle and jeer. It is not a sensible calling.

Some say thoughts are everywhere. Everyone knows what they are and have them all the time. 'I think', is one of the most frequently used phrases in the English language. Isn't it obvious? Well, yes and no. Do you look at thought and ask what it is? Do you ever stare at what you think you know, and wonder if there's something else? Do you push the curtain aside, go backstage, sit in on rehearsals, watch the movements of thought that go into the production of an idea? I do. I have done it for a long time. Sometimes, it seems I have done it all my life, but when we go back far, to beginnings, it can get hazy. But haziness does not now deter me as I sit here in my home in Sydney, Australia, and embark on a writing journey into the essence of thought.

But this is not an account written from armchair reflections. We are beings in a real world, citizens of the earth, and the reality outside is as necessary to engage with as the reality within. I, and the many people who do similar work, have a responsibility to be good psychoanalytic citizens of the world. I was provoked to write by the scandal of clerical child sexual abuse in the Catholic church. Millions of words have already been written about the issue. And when we read and listen, the oxygen can quickly be taken from our minds. As we hear described what a priest did to the body of a child, as we follow the trail of leaders protecting their church like a mafia ruthlessly silencing dissenters, we recoil in horror.

I sensed a duty to write. I also sensed a right to write. But both must give way to a more important reason. I write because I need to write. Writing is, to me, a form of thinking. I had to write about the abuse of children by religious figures because I had questions for which I could not find answers. Writing the truth heals the mind.

Now I go back to my beginnings. Each of us is born into a set of circumstances which shape and define us. I was born into a staunchly Catholic Ireland where God and the devil waged war for your soul. Heaven and hell were places as real as the not-too-distant hills and valleys. When I was eighteen, I read the hellfire and brimstone sermons immortalised by James Joyce in *Portrait of the Artist as a Young Man*. I heard nothing new. When I was eight, I knelt in the pew of the parish church on the first night of the mission as the visiting preacher in flowing black cape walked up the dimly lit aisle, genuflected before the altar, mounted the pulpit and bellowed, 'It is appointed onto men once to die and after that the judgement.'

The first sermon in a mission was always about Hell and Eternal Damnation.

The first principle of the church was, you don't need to think. We'll do it for you. In Catholic Ireland, the big questions of life sat side by side with everyday events. To walk on untarred lanes from home to primary school became a journey into obedience. If, following a local death, you paused in the playground, through the willows in the graveyard next door you could see a gravedigger with crowbar, spade and shovel. On the way back to class, those older dared you to look again. The bones and skull of the previous occupant of the grave sat in a neat pile beside the mound of fresh brown earth. Next year, you did the daring.

In the five years between finishing school and moving to London, I lived in a religious community. This, at the time, seemed a natural progression. I was studying for the priesthood. As a psychoanalyst, I have had direct experience of people who came to me to deal with the trauma of incest and sexual, physical and emotional abuse. As a clinical supervisor, I have listened to numerous accounts of abuse by priests and religious figures. I have also spent considerable time over the years acquainting myself with the writing by others who have put their minds to this issue.

To fill in some gaps and show you in more detail where I have come from, I add the following. When I studied philosophy, the subject that most interested me was epistemology, which is the study of human understanding; how our mind progresses from knowing nothing to knowing something. In fact, my first glimpses of psychoanalysis were through the eyes of the Canadian Jesuit philosopher Bernard Lonergan. I was a social worker in London for seventeen years, first as a community worker in Camden and then a psychiatric social worker in a child guidance clinic in the East End. During those years, I studied in the evenings for an MA in Deviancy and Social Policy (Criminology). Also, in those years I became interested in the work of the Tavistock Clinic, where I studied and would later teach.

So I picked up the pencil and returned to this non-sensible profession because I needed to. In part, I write for myself.

In the privacy of our own mind, the written word makes space. A sentence begins not knowing where it will end. In a tiny, infinitesimal way, the mark of the full stop signifies (if what was made was good) that the writer, by that tiny, infinitesimal measure, has been changed.

But words on pages are gestures of communication, are like hands outstretched, eyes open, expectant. We are social creatures. We exist only because the body of another held us, from nothing to a nine-month-old child ready for life. And that life, we hope, will, when it ceases, cease with those we have loved and who have loved us. Interdependence, communality, togetherness (call it what you like) is fundamental to our existence.

Therefore, in part I write for others.

*

Growing up in a place, you get to hear its history and stories. There was a story in Ireland about a tourist who came to find the Real Old Ireland.

He was driving from Galway to Dublin and left the main highway. On the small country lanes called boreens, he got lost. In the middle of nowhere, with no signposts to guide him, he came across a farmer leaning on a gate. 'Can you tell me how to get from here to Dublin?' he asked, with urgency.

He was answered slowly: 'Now if I was going to Dublin, I wouldn't start from here.'

Having told you why I'm writing this book, I will now tell you where I intend to start. 'Tell all the truth, but tell it slant,' Emily Dickinson said. I have enough of the Irish farmer in my head to tell me to follow my own map. 'Success in circuit lies,' Emily Dickinson (a child of Heraclitus) added. Before I get on the main road that will take us to the big issues, I take a circuitous route through literature. In fact, there will be many times throughout the book where I make such detours. For me, reading literature is like ploughing. Turning the sod is the first essential step to cultivating good soil to grow things. In the good soil of literature, minds grow.

Emily Dickinson is one of many writers you will meet along the way. I will take you back to those who spoke to me, who tapped on the door of my mind through the years since my pencil first contrived to trace diagonals. You may already know their writings, but it's as I have met them along the road of my life, that I will talk of them. They are 'my people'.

Emily Dickinson was a poet who spent a lot of time looking at the stars and saw things few before her had. I step into the light of her mind many times in this book. She worked hard on her poetry (rising in the small hours while the house slept) but one of her lessons is to not tighten the muscles of our minds, to get used to waiting and leave the shooting star to its own devices.

> A thought went up my mind to-day
> That I have had before,
> But did not finish, – some way back,
> I could not fix the year,
> Nor where it went, nor why it came
> The second time to me,
> Nor definitely what it was,
> Have I the art to say.
> But somewhere in my soul, I know
> I've met the thing before
> It just reminded me – 't was all –
> And came my way no more.

*

Poetry is a form of thinking. Poems see into the dark. Poems know best the beat of human heart. I would remain alive without poetry, but I would not be alive. My world would turn monochrome (as would the art lover's without art, or the music lover's should sound cease). The American poet Stanley Kunitz said poetry is the only uncorrupted form of expression because it has no market value. Be prepared. Poems will pop up a lot. They are a backdrop to the many scenes. Sometimes, you will stumble on one but it will go on minding its own business. Also (perhaps in pauses and silences), the poem will take up all the space and speak loudly for itself. I use the poems of others and I use my own.

In October of 2020 (the year Covid-19 etched fear and confusion on the mind of the world) poetry found a new voice – clear and fearless – on the world stage, when Louise Glück was awarded the Nobel Prize for Literature by the Swedish Academy, whose spokesman said, 'her poetry honoured the intimate, private voice, which public utterance can sometimes augment or extend, but never replace'.

Glück's poetry has an austere beauty while her prose displays a razor-sharp mind; her essays (few in number) are compact with searing perception and comprehensive insight and repay hours of contemplation and frequent return.

But it was not always so and her story about her childhood and how she learned to think and found freedom to write is most instructive. She has told it herself in an essay called 'Education of the Poet'.

> At 16…I realised, logically, that to be 85, then 80, then 75 pounds was to be thin; I understood that at some point I was going to die… One day I told my parents I thought I should see a psychoanalyst. I had no idea where the idea, the word came from… I was immensely fortunate in the analyst my parents found. My seven-year analysis taught me to think…taught me to use doubt…it gave me an intellectual task capable of transforming paralysis into insight. It is fortunate that that discipline gave me a place to use my mind, because my emotional condition, my extreme rigidity of behaviour and frantic dependence on ritual, made other forms of education impossible.

*

You may have heard the exchange between the tourist and the Irish farmer told as a joke. It works as one. But like many jokes, turn it on its side or upside down and it reveals something else. I grew up with men like him. Born at the end of the nineteenth or the beginning of the twentieth century, they did not travel far. They knew their own townland like the back of their hands and carried its history in their memory. With little formal education and few books, they nonetheless could read people. And if their lives were local, to the extent that they reached into the inner world, and looked outwards and upwards to the stars, they could touch the universal.

The scandal in the Catholic church is not a subject I can exhaustively attend to (it takes up about one-fifth of the book). It allows entry points into thought, stepping stones towards an exploration of that fascinating place we call the mind. It allows examination of ways in which thought fails, shows minds in disarray. We gain useful understanding when we see more clearly a failure of thought, of ways in which it is disrupted, unlearned, eschewed or perverted. How does a Christian priest who believes his seven-year-old altar boy is created in the image and likeness of God and whose body is a temple of the Holy Spirit, lock the sacristy door after celebrating Mass and rape the child?

Stepping stones convey a sense of solidity and I do my best to provide, if you walk with me, reliable directions. But at some stages it may seem we are standing on a rickety crossing. The only assurance I can here offer is that I have already placed myself on many vertiginous bridges. To raise questions that one is not supposed to raise, and to suggest that some who lay claim to absolute truth may in fact have feet of clay, faith is required, the faith that when you know the elements on offer are inadequate, you carry on in search of the quintessence of thought.

*

A summary of the contents of the book and the direction it takes: it is in three parts. Part one continues in the next chapter highlighting the importance of language. Debase language and you debase thought. Part one continues with an imaginary letter to the world today by one of the great thinkers of the twentieth century, Sigmund Freud. Then it enters an area where I suggest there is a collapse of thought: the spiritual chaos in the Catholic church associated with clerical child sexual abuse.

Part two is devoted to writers who impress, not only because of *what* they say but how they say it, how they offer access to their minds. As they write, they show you *how* they think. The American poet Emily Dickinson, the Irish novelist John McGahern, the English essayist William Hazlitt stand out. There are also chapters on dreaming and spirituality.

Part three does not try to sum up and reach a conclusion. The chapters are shorter and have an overall design, but can be read in any order. They are like a bracelet of short stories or poems that circle a theme. They are stepping stones leading beyond the familiar possibilities of thought renewed.

2

The Rough Magic of Words

In 1912 at Place de la Concorde on the Paris Metro, Ezra Pound watched the passing flow of faces. He wrote a poem. The poem was thirty lines. He was unhappy with what he'd written; the words had failed to capture the experience. He carried the thirty lines around for six months. He rewrote the poem. The new poem was fifteen lines. Another six months passed. Still unhappy, he pared the poem down and found the words that were sufficient to capture what he had experienced. Two lines. Fourteen words.

I focus here not on the poem itself but the process of writing. Pound said that writing such short poems was a risky activity; the poem may seem meaningless. I agree with Pound that it is risky. We can examine the nature of the risk. A poem is not life; life and poetry are different. They have different kinds of existence. A poem will draw inspiration from life, sail close to life, run parallel to life, but if they collide, the poem is no longer a poem. A poem is a thing. Edward Hirsch called it 'a made thing'.

In 1585, another poet, Edward Dyer, wrote,

> My mind to me a kingdom is,
> Such present joy therein I find,
> That it excels all other bliss
> That earth affords or grows by kind.

Ezra Pound held his experience at Place de la Concorde inside the kingdom of his mind for a year before offering us his poem. If, having lived inside the kingdom of his mind, the poet offers us his poem, do we receive it into the kingdom of our mind? The telling of this story about poetry presents two fundamental challenges: do we treat a poem as a thing; do we take it into the kingdom of our mind?

These little poems require a lot of the reader. They raise big questions. The writer risks packing something so tight it can't be unpacked. The reader is challenged to make more of him or herself available to explore and then extend the poem. I once pared a poem down to ten words. I named it 'Real Presence'.

> Your spirit at my side
> absent footprints
> in the snow.

*

In this book, I offer many signposts which might at first seem confusing. But the Irish direction-provider is more than a quaint speaker. When lost, I say, go back to the local. It's the best place to start. Because of influences that shaped me, when I get lost, I turn to literature. Poetry has always helped. My first encounter with poetry was in a two-roomed, two-teacher primary school, built in 1830 in an enclosure with a church and churchyard. Thomas Gray could have written his 'Elegy' at dusk under the willows. His thoughts and ideas challenged; the rhythm of his words the rhythm of my heartbeat. Yeats's terrible beauty was born in this land and if you lifted your eyes you could see his nine-and-fifty swans fly from Coole. I don't remember when I first heard about William Shakespeare. He seemed to have always been there. His 'thou' and 'thee' and 'canst not' not strange to my ear, perhaps because it had been tuned by the Bible to such words.

Poems, in my 1950s Ireland, were learned by heart. Corporal punishment was practised. But somehow any threat of the rod diminished in the face of a love for the thing itself. I found that poetry was alone in that it never condemned nor threatened to condemn, never instilled fear or badness. It did not offer escape and transportation to perfection, but it did lift you out of grey and colourless days and suggested beauty might touch the local and the everyday. Poetry, back then, seemed to belong to the earth: sky, trees, flowers, birds, animals, the land itself, everything that made your world human, belonged to poetry. I could not have said that then. Even now, as I write it, half of me has moved beyond the horizon of what I see.

The boy observing life; the man observing the boy.

In my published novel called *Boat People*, I imagined I was back in the two-teacher school. I went beyond my own time, back to 1830. I imagined the first schoolmaster – I called him Donald Pendergast – address his young pupils, helping them survive in a harsh world. Master Pendergast told them, 'A poem is the most useless and useful thing you will ever know. It's worth nothing and everything. Learn to read and think about a poem: you will be able to think about anything.'

That story, the novel began in 1848. The Great Famine has devastated Ireland. The Donavan family – Michael the father and Catherine the mother, and their daughters Aoifa and Emily, prepare to emigrate to Australia. They close their cottage door for the last time. They travel by pony and trap.

> They passed along the hedgerows where Michael had played as a child. When he was a small boy he knew the position of every bird's nest along the way: the thrush; the blackbird; the robin. He knew them all by the colour of their eggs. And the wren, the smallest of all, the only one to put a roof on its house. When Catherine came to these parts she too walked the fields, first with Michael, then with growing life in her womb. Later, before Aoifa and Emily had grown steady on their feet, each were lifted and invited to look into secret places and see those priceless treasures: the eggs of the thrush, blue with browney-red speckles; those of the blackbird, a turquoisy-blue; the robin red-breast's pale bluish-green. Days later they looked again and saw and heard the tiny, blind chicks. Outside the nest the discarded pieces of egg-shell were carefully picked up and carried home in the palm of the hand.
>
> Mrs Fingleton stood at the end of her laneway; her grandson

at her side. She looked like some ancient building; he a flying buttress holding her erect. Michael saw her battle with pain as she stood and waited... The old woman spoke in the old Gaelic tongue.

> *Go n-éirí an bóthar leat*
> *Go raibh an ghaoth go brách ag do chúl*
> *Go lonraí an ghrian go te ar d'aghaidh*
> *Go dtite an bháisteach go mín ar do pháirceanna*
> *Agus go mbuailimid le chéile arís,*
> *Go gcoinní Dia i mbos A láimhe thú.*

Before they had gone half a mile they had passed fields, each with their own name, each telling a history which was never written down. The Grove, Murphy's, the Larches, the Rath, the Copse, the Hollow. And each twist or turn along the road, each small stream crossed had its history and its name.

Out of the misty morning a spectral figure emerged, walking towards them on the side of the road. Michael knew him by his step. They had sat beside each other and shared the same slate in Donald Pendergast's classroom. Like a hooded shade he raised his arm straight up, high above his shoulder, his head bowed. For him all goodbyes had been spoken, all looks given and received. He neither slowed down nor increased his speed, but walked steadily on, his arm still held high, as the mist, having momentarily presented him, received him back again.

What do we notice as we pass through life? What do we see? What do we hear, listen for? As we migrate, through a day, a week, a year, what happens to us? Do we have the spirits of others at our side? Are we aware of the absent footprints? Do we stare long enough to see something that means something? Will we spend months, years, living with a fleeting moment?

Loss follows us wherever we go. There are big losses and small losses. It might seem a very small loss, but I lost a word for forty years. Didn't know it was gone; it just fell off. When I was preparing to talk about *Boat People* to an audience in Perth, I tripped over it.

The first lines of what Mrs Fingleton said – *Go n-éirí an bóthar leat?/ Go raibh an ghaoth go brách ag do chúl* – translate as 'May the road rise to meet you / May the wind be always at your back.' I had written those words into the text of the novel and silently read them many times through various drafts to galley proofs and finally as printed book. But it was not until I was preparing my thoughts for the Perth launch that I spoke them aloud in Gaelic. Halfway through the second line. I was overcome by the sound of the word *ghaoth*.

Speaking and hearing the word *ghaoth* after forty years of silence I wept. *Ghaoth* means wind; *an ghaoth*, the wind. It is spelt *g h a o t h*. In Gaelic, 'h' after a letter softens it. The Gaelic alphabet has eighteen letters. There is no English 'th' sound (as in 'those' or 'this') in Gaelic. So, the 'g' and 'th' are softened: *ghaoth*. It is pronounced g'way. The word onomatopoeic; the sound of a passing breeze.

I tripped over *ghaoth* and I was undone.

This is an example of a single word that got lost and lay dormant in an individual for decades. It was a word in a poem. The Gaelic blessing is a poem. It might be called a Gaelic psalm.

As a writer, I use poetry and prose in tandem. I often find writing a poem the best way to advance something that I am working on in a novel. I'm not talking about what ends up on the page, but about the preparatory work that takes place before the final text is ready. It's the practice of taking something you are struggling to know, into a different form of expression, and see what happens. It could also be described as plugging into the power of the poem – the power that made thing, that made-up-thing, can have. It is the energy Seamus Heaney described (in his Nobel Literature Prize lecture, *The Redress of Poetry*) as 'the power to persuade that vulnerable part of our consciousness of its rightness… that our solitudes and distresses are creditable…parts of being a human being.'

Emboldened by Heaney, I persuaded myself to attempt to articulate further what I had stumbled upon when *ghaoth* appeared from my past. But rather than think it out, I wrote it out. (Out, in the sense, out of me.) But as I can never 'decide' to write a poem, I just left the impulse there, to mind its own business, and got on with mine.

It started. I built it around an old sixteenth-century Gaelic poem called '*Cill Cháis*' (pronounced Kilcash). '*Cill Cháis*' was translated into English by the Irish poet Thomas Kinsella. The poem was also set to music and was sung in both languages, so it offered a rich cauldron of possibilities.

'*Cill Cháis*' was the name of a large estate near Clonmel in County Tipperary and was owned by the Butler family. The poem was written partly as a lament on the death of a much-loved woman, Margaret Butler. It also laments the destruction of the old local forests. The bell in the poem was like an old clock – used to sound the work hours of the day.

Anglo Irish

I never learned the Gaelic tongue
with any fluency but of late
long-forgotten words
old songs
poems
visit in the night.

Deep inside me the poem-songs sing
like summer leaves shimmering in the trees
like autumn leaves rustling under my feet.

Cad a dhéanfaimid feasta gan adhmad?
Tá deireadh na gcoillte ar lár;
níl trácht ar Chill Cháis ná ar a teaghlach
is ní bainfear a cling go bráth.

Thomas Kinsella translated the Gaelic
words of the unknown bard:
'Now what will we do for timber,
with the last of the woods laid low?
There's no talk of Kilcash or its household
and its bell will be struck no more.'

Lost words lost worlds
one and the same
languages like tall trees
drive roots
deep into the soil of the mind
the silent bell tolls for the silent voice.

One man's gibberish
is to another's ear
sweet music
the score
written in his mother's eyes
her voice the bow
that moved from string to string.

Melodies now wander
in the twilight of my mind
calling me
to the dawn
to my creation
the moment when sounds
sang their way
into the marrow
of my soul.

*

Language is one of the most exquisite human inventions. It is pivotal to our humanness. The word 'human' would mean something utterly different without language. The Orkney writer George Mackay Brown wrote,

> If language is lost word and name are drained of their ancient power. It is the word, blossoming as legend, poem, story, secret, that holds a community together and gives meaning to its life. If words become functional ciphers merely…they lose their 'ghosts' – the rich aura that has grown around them from the start, and grows infinitesimally richer every time they are spoken. They lose

their 'kernel', the sheer sensuous relish of utterance. Poetry is a fine interpenetration of ghost and kernel. We are in danger of contenting ourselves with husks. Decay of language is always the symptom of a more serious sickness.

As we combat those who embrace 'alternative facts' and debase truth and language, we need to be well armed. Language expresses, and communicates. And it touches that which in inexpressible, just like music. James Joyce spoke about a piano being a coffin of notes. It needed a pianist to make the music live. John McGahern extended the analogy to a book which he said was a coffin of words. It needed a reader to make the words live.

Emily Dickinson, the mistress of succinctness, said,

> A word is dead
> When it is said
> Some say – I say
> It just begins
> To live that day.

One of the articles of faith in the kingdom of my writing mind is expressed by Prospero in *The Tempest*:

> we are such stuff
> As dreams are made on

Without night dreams and daydreams, we would all be lost in a strange world called 'reality'. There would be no imagination. In the mind of the writer, the world of the imagination is as real as the chair you sit on. The creation of a poem or a novel or any work of fiction is the creation of a dream space into which the listener and reader are invited.

If you look out for Mackay Brown's 'ghosts', or listen to the melodies in the twilight of your mind, it can have a knock-on effect. Once in there, a process can take over. It's hard to describe or explain but I have found myself writing other poems that must be somehow unconsciously provoked. This is one such poem.

Perfect Pitch

It happened impromptu
when the word impromptu
was beyond me.
People would call to the house
there'd be talk
of the weather
of rheumatism and lumbago
of who had died
and who had lately
come into the world.

The violin case would open
the melodeon taken from its box
tin whistles from the shelf.
Speech would cease.
Eyes close
and voices turn to song.

That was fifty years ago.
And today
I wait in silence and when I hear
the perfect pitch of stillness
I know the bow is on the string
fingers caress the keys, eyes
are closing and heaven's gate
is opening once again.

    In our individual development, I would suggest we all begin with the poetic. We learn and appreciate elements of the poetic before we learn and appreciate the elements of prose. Observe a parent and infant in that long period before a child utters its first sentence. The child first hears the music of language, the emotion that is carried by the sound of the voice and the words. We dream before we speak.

Upon these early aural foundations, we construct a whole edifice of sound. There are the human voices and accents that surround us. There is much variation here: London, Yorkshire, Sydney, Glasgow, the Bronx, Ireland, have different accents. All speak English.

We each have our own private orchestral history: human sounds; nature's sounds. A screeching kookaburra's; the crek-crek call of a corncrake. If you were brought up near a Buddhist temple, the gong announcing dawn and the chanting of the monks would have entered into your very personal internal musical vocabulary. If your place of birth was Catholic Ireland in the 1950s, you'd have had the repetitious incantation of the rosary.

Language drives roots deep into the soil of our minds. When Seamus Heaney was asked by Denis O'Driscoll if he was like Wordsworth, 'who early in life had an intense experience…about inanimate nature which he spent…his poetical life trying to describe,', Heaney said,

> The early-in-life experience has been central to me all right. But I'd say you aren't so much trying to describe it as trying to locate it. The amount of sensory material stored up or stored down in the brain's and the body's systems is inestimable. It's like a culture at the bottom of a jar, although it doesn't grow, I think, or help anything else to grow unless you find a way to reach it and touch it. But once you do, it's like putting your hand into a nest and finding something beginning to hatch out in your hand.

I think of the writer delving into his own mind in this way. He does this work in the making of a poem or a novel. Heaney wrote a poem called 'The Diviner' and talked of 'poetry as divination; poetry as revelation of the self to the self'. His diviner with the hazel rod finds the hidden treasures. Others want to have a go. He gives them the stick without saying a word. He doesn't need to speak. He has said all he needs to say in the poem.

The reader needs the sound of the poet's poem to plumb his own private depths. Seamus Heaney is a significant figure in my story about poetry. Although ten years my senior and growing up in the North, and

I in the Republic, the Ireland he wrote about was my Ireland. I knew the land, the trees, the birds, the hedgerows, the light, the greenness he knew.

In *Crediting Poetry,* Heaney referred to the

> temple inside our hearing which the passage of the poem calls into being… It has as much to do with the energy released by linguistic fission and fusion, with the buoyancy generated by cadence and tone and rhyme and stanza, as it has to do with the poem's concerns or the poet's truthfulness.

*

I may have lost a single word for decades, but sometimes a word can get lost for centuries. John McGahern told a story about his local football team. Whenever the backs made a relieving clearance. the bystanders shouted out 'Salamanca'. No one knew why, until a link was made to Salamanca in Spain. where young men went to train as priests and secretly returned to Ireland in defiance of the British government. McGahern re-imagined all this and wrote,

> the word Salamanca, having lived for most of a century as a mighty ball booted on the wind out of defence in Charlie's field grew sails again on an open sea, became a walled city with spires in the sun.

So, like *ghaoth* or 'Salamanca', emotionally powered words don't become extinct. They become unconscious. They hibernate. They are carried inside individuals and in communities. It is probable that many emotionally powered words are laid down within us when we are children, particularly when we can hear but have not yet learned to speak. When we meet them again, we have to sound them, to hear them, to know them.

Ted Hughes wrote about our 'musical or audial memory', about verbal sounds automatically linking up to root words that are beyond immediate awareness or conscious manifestation. 'There are,' he said, 'vast systems of root meanings and related associations in the deep subsoil of psychological life. And it is the hidden patterns that are the stronger.' T.S. Eliot wrote about plumbing the depths of 'the auditory imagination'. Eliot observed that a person can know what a poem is about before they understand it.

As a writer of poetry and of prose, I am always aware the reader has his or her own store of powerful words, sounds that await activation. I write poetry to be read out loud. But even in a novel, which for the most part is read silently, I am aware of the silent sound of the music of the words, the cadence of the sentence, the rhythms of the language. I always read my own prose out loud, to check if the music of the language is right. I need to satisfy myself that it is in order. 'Heard melodies are sweet,' John Keats wrote, 'but those unheard are sweeter.'

The writer needs to know the secret musicality of his own particular, peculiar, personal, idiosyncratic way with words. He has to have his own 'musical' house in order. William Hazlitt wrote,

> Most men's minds are like musical instruments out of tune. Touch a particular key and it jars and makes harsh discord with your own.

Silence and stillness are two of life's precious qualities. In today's world where frenzied communication is god, they are rare commodities; where the fast-paced, adrenalin-driven novel can sell millions, there is no place to pause, let alone stop, to let the reader relax, to experience stillness. When you can live with silence and stillness, your words find a hidden key, and everything you hear and speak changes. Stillness isn't a static place where nothing happens. Silence makes room for imagination, inspiration and the capacity to listen.

*

The 'rough magic' in this chapter title is borrowed from Shakespeare's last play, *The Tempest*. Take a giant leap. Imagine being Shakespeare. You are in the shoes of a man who knows the true value of his work, who believes his poems and plays will be read and performed well into the future. You might even anticipate that an authority on literature will, sometime in the future, say that you wrote plays that 'abide beyond the edge of the mind's reach, [and] remain the outward limit of human achievement' (Harold Bloom). You decide at age forty-seven to stop writing. You are planning your final play. Will you rest on your laurels or do something totally different?

The storyline of *The Tempest* is simple. A magician called Prospero lives on an enchanted island with his daughter Miranda and two others; Caliban is half-savage and is Prospero's slave; Ariel is a spirit who also serves Prospero. Prospero was Duke of Milan. His brother Antonio usurped his position and drove Prospero into exile. Antonio is on a ship near the island. Prospero intent on revenge creates a tempest to force his brother and the ship's crew onto the island. There are various stands to the story as the newcomers interact with the residents. Perhaps predictably, Prospero forgives his brother and he is restored to his dukedom.

But unpredictably, Shakespeare creates a character unlike any in all his previous plays. *Hamlet, Lear, Macbeth, Othello, Cleopatra* and others live in the minds of many. Some of their words, like Hamlet's 'To be, or not to be', easily recognisable. But in his final work, Shakespeare does something totally different. He creates Ariel, unique among the hundreds of his previous characters.

When the play is staged, the part of Ariel can be played by a male or female actor. Ariel is hard to pin down. Ariel is not human. Who is he/she/it? In the play, Ariel is often an invisible or disguised presence. If we listen to the story of *The Tempest*, we hear that Ariel was imprisoned by the witch Sycorax in a cloven pine for twelve years. Sycorax, who was Caliban's mother, controlled the island before Prospero's arrival. She incarcerated Ariel because Ariel was

> A spirit too delicate
> To act her earthly and abhorn'd commands.

Sycorax however was powerless to release Ariel. It was Prospero's magic that enabled release. Ariel was then in Prospero's service. Prospero created the tempest to trap his enemies but when anything subtle was required, he called upon Ariel. Ariel guided the crew to safety. Ariel sent people to sleep. Ariel made the music and the dance and when required improvised. Prospero wished his daughter Miranda to fall in love with Ferdinand but bringing that about was Ariel's work. And Ariel's music is the spontaneous overflow of the joy of life.

Harold Goddard in *The Meaning of Shakespeare* conceived of the interactions between Sycorax, Prospero and Ariel as an allegory. In the allegory, Ariel is Imagination; Sycorax represents the Senses; Prospero represents Reason. When enslaved by the senses, superstition dominates and thinking function and the senses become powerless to release and use imagination. A totalitarian mind, like that of the witch Sycorax, is utterly devoid of imagination. Reason and knowledge – Prospero was a learned man – came to the rescue and freed up imagination. That's the essence of the allegory.

Prospero's renouncing of his rough magic at the end of the play coincides with the release of Ariel. Music replaces magic. Wonder in the ordinary replaces the performance of wonders. Ariel achieving freedom is pivotal. Ariel is the agent of internal miracles. He is the one who prompts Prospero towards forgiveness. Listen to the way Ariel speaks to Prospero when Prospero asks about his old friend Gonzalo:

> Ariel: His tears run down his beard like winter's drops
> From eaves of reeds. Your charm so strongly works them
> That if you now beheld them, your affections
> Would become tender.
> Prospero: Dost thou think so, spirit?
> Ariel: Mine would, sir, were I human.
> Prospero: And mine shall.

Ariel's magic is life-enhancing. Ariel is present is every act of redemption, reconciliation, compassion and creativity.

Perhaps all poets wait for Ariel's presence at their side. There is stillness and a quietness about Ariel, a stillness and a quietness that is only to be found in the ordinary and the everyday. Ariel's transition at the end takes place quietly. When Prospero gives up his magic, he goes with a flourish. (In one stage production, his book ignited into flames.) In the midst of busy talk about 'important' issues by others on the stage, the final words between Prospero and Ariel are whispered as an aside:

> Then to the elements be free, and fare thou well.

The stage play ends with Prospero's Epilogue. But I think of Shakespeare's last play as having two endings, the other – more important one – is when Ariel makes his exit. Ariel is the imaginative, inventive spirit of Shakespeare. It's his legacy to us. His great works only become great to us when we receive them with our imaginative, inventive mind. This Ariel, this spirit, exists quietly and works its wonders internally. Its fine magic uses simple words, the words of poetry, which will, no matter how dark the world becomes, continue to shine a light, a light that will lead us to the place Miranda described when she saw people she had never seen before.

> O, wonder!
> How many goodly creatures are there here!
> How beauteous man kind is! O brave new world,
> That has such people in 't!

*

At the beginning of this book, I invited you on a journey and promised to introduce you to those whom I called 'my people', those writers, living and dead who have enriched my life. I have introduced some and others will follow. It is important to say that when I turn to them my interest is twofold. Firstly, I want to know what he or she has to say. Secondly, I wish to observe how his or her mind works. I spend a lot of time rereading the same piece often if the writer reveals his or her mind within the writing. Happiness, John McGahern said, writes white: its strength resides in its invisibility; you don't achieve it by chasing after it. Writers who reveal their mind's workings don't generally shout about it. Like happiness, it is written white. And we need to want to know.

Poetry and the language of rational thought are separate and distinct branches of authorship and yet they constantly overlap and intermingle. I use my own poems to illustrate, to show what I cannot show in any other way. Some poems were written independent of this book. Others I wrote when prose words were beyond me, or I simply knew that the best way to speak was through a poem. An index and a list of references are provided but no footnotes or endnotes. Where a poem by someone else is cited, their name will be given. The Internet is a pathway to the libraries of the world where a name or a quotation can be followed up. All uncited poems are mine.

3

An Education in Thinking

I became interested in psychoanalysis because I needed to learn how to think. I first experienced a real liberation of the mind while I studied philosophy at Milltown Park, the Jesuit College in Dublin. My first introduction to Freud was, as I have already said, through the Jesuit philosopher Bernard Lonergan's book *Insight: A Study of Human Understanding*. But I already knew instinctively, if not explicitly, that there was a thinking beyond (or other than) the 'cerebral', and beyond the 'spiritual'. Heaney's *The Redress of Poetry* was many years into the future, but it would prove to have the words I was leaning towards:

> the power to persuade that vulnerable part of our consciousness of its rightness...that our solitudes and distresses are creditable...parts of being a human being.

Written, but not then read by me, were the words of Marcel Proust:

> Most of our attempts to translate our innermost feelings do no more than relieve us of them by drawing them out in a blurred form which does not help us to identify them.

In 1895, the first psychoanalyst, Sigmund Freud, stopped thinking like a doctor and started thinking like a poet. *Studies in Hysteria* was published that year and a reviewer wrote,

> We do not know how science will judge the theories of Breuer and Freud, but they have the poets on their side, and that means a great deal. For us yet the poets have been those who knew best about the secrets of the human soul.

In 1994, at the Sydney Institute for Psychoanalysis, the visiting American psychoanalyst John Gedo gave a public lecture. The lively question and answer time which followed glided into a quieter and reflective mood. Asked if he could distil the essence of psychoanalysis into a single sentence, Gedo, after at least a full minute's silence, said psychoanalysis is an education in thinking.

In 2008, the Nicholson Museum at the University of Sydney hosted an exhibition entitled *Sigmund Freud's Collection: An Archaeology of the Mind*. In his lifelong fascination with archaeology, he collected many small objects. The collection is permanently stored at the Freud Museum in London, where in his study/consulting room, the objects and Freud's books compete for available space. Nineteen of these objects were on loan to the Nicholson. The museum also organised a series of lectures and, as chairman of the Sydney Institute for Psychoanalysis, I was invited to give the opening lecture. I decided on an unfamiliar form of presentation. I imagined what Freud might say, were he to write to the world today. Freud was a good writer and often adopted the style of a conversationalist speaking directly to an audience. This, his/my 'letter', uses some of his actual words, some of my own clinical experiences.

*

Dear Friends of the Nicholson, ladies and gentlemen, I see we are in the twenty-first century. Next year will be the sixtieth anniversary of my death. I'd hoped to end my days in my native Vienna but hate and intolerance drove me out. At the age of eighty-two I became a refugee. I spent the final year of my life in London, where I died on September 23rd 1939. I see you have around you many images, still and moving images of my life and my home in Vienna. Before I vacated my rooms and left them to the mercies of the Gestapo, a photographer Edmund Engelman secretly used the magic of his camera to record the space in which I worked for fifty years. My couch has been faithfully presented and above all you have here a fine selection of my beloved archaeological objects.

I pondered before picking up my pen, to consider what to say to the world. I could point you to the twenty-four volumes of my collected psychological papers or to the numerous biographies written about me. The International Psychoanalytical Association founded at Salzburg in 1908 has today some 11,000 members on all parts of the globe. Every library around the world will have some book or mention of me and my ideas. Apart from those who still continue with the clinical practice which I invented, there are countless forms of psychotherapy based on my ideas. In addition, every aspect of the arts and humanities and the social sciences have been shaped for better or worse by my writings.

When in 1993 *Time* magazine had a cover photo of me with the question 'Is Freud Dead', you can appreciate why I had a slight chuckle.

You will be pleased to know that I'm not going to instruct you to read. Instead I am going to ask something of you. As you will know, when a patient came to see me, I invited them to lie on my couch. I sat in a chair at the head of the couch. What I now want to ask of you is this: I invite you to sit in my chair. Go on, humour an old man. If you want to know me, put yourself in my place.

Settle yourself in; look around. In my rooms in Vienna and in London, when I sat in my chair, I was surrounded by my archaeological collection. There were 1,000 pieces in my room; fifty on my desk alone. Imagine you are sitting among them. Each and every piece has its own history. They had been collected over a period of fifty years. When I sat among them, I enjoyed their presence, their stillness. I felt in touch with the people who made those small objects thousands of years ago. People who reached out and took into their hands inert material and gave it a shape, gave it beauty, meaning, created art.

While I sat and looked around, the past and the great stories and human challenges that encircle these objects seemed to flow around me and pass through me. Imagine you are alone with them; that the space in which you sit and work and write and think is filled with them. I loved those pieces. Collecting them over a lifetime gave me great pleasure.

There is another part on my working space that you need to know about if you are to enter into the spirit of our little game. My books, all 3,600 of them, lined the shelves and walls of my rooms. My earlier advice to hold off reaching for a book was not meant to discourage you from reading. Reading was one of the great pleasures of my life. I'll tell you two little stories about books.

In 1906, Hugo Heller, a Viennese bookseller, wrote to me and to other well-known people and asked us to name 'ten good books'. I was unclear what he meant by the word 'good'. I wrote back and asked if he meant the ten most magnificent works of world literature, in which case we would be talking of Homer, the tragedies of Sophocles, Goethe's *Faust*, Shakespeare's *Hamlet*, *Macbeth*, et cetera. I also wondered if 'good' really meant significant. If so, we would have to start with Copernicus, with Darwin's *Descent of Man*, I said to him also that if by 'good' he meant my favourites, Milton's *Paradise Lost* and Heine's *Lazarus* would be top of my list.

Well, as you can see, ladies and gentlemen, I took a little detour before I got to answer his question. I rather liked detours. You never know what you stumble upon. Anyway, I proceeded with the task. You see I read widely. My ten authors were of seven nationalities: Dutch, English, French, Russian, Swiss, Austrian and American. I spoke and read in a number of languages. My list of ten good books included two novels, a biography, imaginary correspondence, a cycle of poems, novellas, a collection of humorous sketches, stories about savage animals and little less-savage men, formal essays, and a history of Greek philosophy. My writers included Mark Twain, Macaulay, Anatole France, Kipling, Zola, Keller, Mayer and Dekker.

My second story concerns the writer Arthur Schnitzler. Like me, he trained as a doctor and a neurologist but he gave them up and spent his life writing literature. When he was sixty, I wrote to him to wish him long life and I said the following:

I think I have avoided you from a kind of awe of meeting my double...whenever I get deeply interested in your beautiful creations I always seem to find behind their poetic sheen the same pre-suppositions, interests and conclusions as those familiar to me as my own...your deep grasp of the truths of the unconscious...the way you take to pieces the social conventions of our society, and the extent to which your thoughts are preoccupied with the polarity of love and death; all that moves me with an uncanny feeling of familiarity. So...you know through intuition – really from a delicate self-observation – everything that I have discovered in other people by laborious work. Indeed, I believe that fundamentally you are an explorer of the depths, as honestly impartial and unperturbed as ever anyone was.

What am I saying to you, ladies and gentlemen? I'm saying that my ideas were the fruit of much reading. I'm saying that my psychoanalysis drew on the wisdom of the great writers and thinkers. The review of *Studies in Hysteria* said we had the poets on our side and 'the poets have been those who knew best about the secrets of the human soul'.

Having talked about my books, let me return for a moment to my archaeological collection. They were all very old: Syrian, Egyptian, Etruscan, Greek, Roman and Chinese.

So, on the one hand, we have the books full of ideas, words, language, thoughts, concepts; a great store of human rationality. And on the other hand, all these objects, many made before the written word existed, before there was an alphabet. No written words. No words to pass to posterity. The image, the shape, the touch is everything.

Here, in the middle of those worlds, between the sophistication of language and mute humanity, between them I placed my chair. And my couch. I saw that world between rationality and art, between the organised coherent place of words, and the place before words and beyond words. I saw that in-between place. I didn't invent it. The poets and writers pointed me to it. The great writers showed the way: Schnitzler knew that world. Shakespeare, Goethe, Dostoyevsky knew it. Their familiarity with the complexity of the human mind, their knowledge, their wisdom, underpinned my psychology. They knew about that in-between world. Great writers knew how to enter that world. The English essayist William Hazlitt wrote,

> There is a method of tying periods on the ear, or weighing them with the scales of the breath, without any articulate sound.' Authors, as they write may be said to 'hear a sound so fine, there's nothing lives 'twixt it and silence'.

But while I owe all these writers a great debt, I did something of my own, something original, and something that no one had done before me. I found a new way to allow entry into that world and by entering into that world, that space I created the means by which human beings can know themselves.

And so, to the next step. This you must take if you are to fully understand what I am talking about: you need to lie on the couch. Use that most wonderful of human faculties, your imagination. Lie back. Allow yourself to enter into that in-between world.

I will tell you another little story that may help. When I was thirteen, I was given a book as a gift. It was a collection of essays written in 1823 by the writer Ludwig Borne. Borne gave advice to a writer on how to write imaginatively. He said,

> Take a few sheets of paper and for three days on end write down, without fabrication or hypocrisy everything that comes into your head. Write down what you think of yourself, of your wife, of the Turkish War, of Goethe, of the Last Judgement, of your superiors – and when three days have passed you will be quite out of your senses with astonishment at the new and un-heard-of thoughts you have had. This is the art of becoming an original writer in three days.

Ladies and gentlemen, when I was sixty-three, I took that little book of essays off my shelf and reread it. I was amazed how much in it agreed practically word for word with things I have always maintained and thought. I have Borne to thank for what I believe was my truly original action, that chair and that couch. You see, that's precisely what I said to my patients when I invited them to lie on the couch.

It's what psychoanalysts the world over still asks of their patients: speak about whatever comes spontaneously to mind. We put so much value on rational thought and think we are masters of our own destiny but alas we are not. It is not easy to relax the censorship that we and society have imposed. It's hard to let thoughts and words come freely without fabrication or hypocrisy. But it's the key that allows you to enter another world. Saying what comes to your mind spontaneously allows you to inhabit a new world. It opens a gateway which Shakespeare signalled at the end of *The Tragedy of King Lear.*

> The weight of this sad time we must obey,
> Speak what we feel, not what we ought to say.

*

A woman walked into a psychoanalyst's consulting room. She moved slowly. She looked stunned. When the psychoanalyst had opened the door of the building to let her in, he spoke his own name. She said nothing. The psychoanalyst gestured towards a chair. She sat. When she had telephoned to make the appointment, she conveyed very little. 'I have some…difficulties. I need someone…to talk to.'

It was usual for the psychoanalyst to ask the patient why they had come, but something told him to hold off. The woman sat forward on the edge of the chair and stared at the analyst.

Staring evokes many different emotions, often anxious ones. In this instance, he experienced no anxiety and was content with being looked at this way. He looked back, but did not stare. If his own thoughts about where he was and who he was with progressed better by looking down or gazing nowhere, he allowed this to happen.

Fifteen minutes passed.

The woman sighed. She said, 'I suppose I should tell you why I came.'

While he waited, the psychoanalyst gave no thought to making possible formulations about what might be transpiring. That came later. He just waited.

*

A man who has been seeing an analyst for some time arrives ten minutes late, lies on the couch and says, 'Sorry, late again.'

What the analyst said in response to those three words requires some background briefing.

Words like this had been spoken many times; as lateness had crept in, apologies were frequent. Sorry had been said many times, with varying degrees of contriteness, frustration, anger – in fact, a whole array of emotions. But this time, the analyst heard something else.

The analyst said, 'The sound of this "sorry" is different from anything I have heard before. I'm sitting here and I'm slowing down what I heard. I heard you say sorry to me. You and I had arranged to meet at eight a.m. I waited for you. You came late. You told me you were sorry.'

But there is another part to this story. When the words 'late again' were spoken, another sound was heard, a discordant note. A voice off-key. The sound was similar to hearing a poem read aloud where a single word grated. The poet, by being rushed or misguided perhaps, had not taken the time to listen to the music of the words.

What the analyst added will make this clearer.

'But I have to add that when you said "late again", you made reference to an unknown number of other times when you were late. I think you stopped yourself listening to that single word you spoke to me. So, I'm curious, because it seems to me that as soon as you expressed sorrow, you took it back again.'

'I think,' the man says, 'there is something in that. I'm fed up today. I didn't want to come.'

*

A year into seeing an analyst, a woman who was normally very talkative fell silent. Fifteen minutes passed. The analyst is puzzled, tries to listen, quietly, but new events always present a challenge. The analyst is pulled back in time, back to the days he was a patient, to days when words seemed useless things, where any intelligible utterance was far away and the few clumsy words within reach, were, by some invisible, godlike presence, forbidden. Maybe something should be said.

Something like patience wins. Nothing is said.

Ten more minutes pass.

The woman stirs and speaks. 'I've just realised something. For the past year, I have been talking over myself. I have never stopped and really listened, ever, really listened to myself.' There was a long pause. 'It's true. I have done it all my life.'

The analyst thinks he is a lucky man. He has been present at a moment of creation. When any person speaks what they feel, not what they ought to say, they become more real.

These are instances of what I am talking about.

*

Without fabrication or hypocrisy, what answer would you give to these questions? Do you listen to yourself? Do you listen to other people? Do you think about other people?

My life took a particular turn when I began to listen to myself. After my father died, I put aside an hour a day when I lay on the couch. Listening, whether to oneself or another person, is a rare commodity. My chair and my couch fostered listening inside that in-between world. It's a delicate business. The whole enterprise requires of you that you become a poet. Not that you have to write the poetry, but it's like being out in the country in the early morning and suddenly you see a spider's web glistening with dewdrops. If you have a poet in you, you will stop and stare and wonder. You'll retrace your steps and turn your head and gaze upon those delicate, invisible fibres; beauty suspended on a fine thread. You will delay whatever it was you were rushing on to because you have stumbled on something far more important. What I say to the world today is, listen to the poets; listen to the poetry within yourself; look for the poetry in other people.

Some say that the life of a psychoanalyst is a lonely business. Let me read for you what one of the early English analysts Ella Sharpe, a great lover of poetry, had to say about her life and work.

> From the limited confines of an individual life, limited in time and space and environment, I experience a rich variety of living through my work. I contact all sorts and kinds of living, all imaginable circumstances, human tragedy and human comedy, humour and dourness, the pathos of the defeated, the incredible endurances and victories that some souls achieve over human fate. Perhaps for this I personally am most glad I made my choice of psychoanalysis, the rich variety of every type of human experience that has become part of me, that never would have been mine either to experience or to understand in a single mortal life, but for my work.

Friends of the Nicholson, ladies and gentlemen, I said something that my detractors and also some of my followers seem to forget. I said that

> Psychoanalysis is not…a system starting out from a few sharply defined fundamental concepts, seeking to grasp the whole universe with the help of these and, once it is completed, having no room for fresh discoveries. On the contrary, it keeps close to the facts in its field of study, seeks to solve the immediate problems of observation, gropes its way forward by the help of experience, is always incomplete and always ready to correct or modify its theories.

Theories are like wine bottles. They're necessary but it is what is inside that is of real value. Listening is the foundation of self-knowledge. A chair, a couch, a person having regular and frequent times to enter into that world allows all manner of things to be listened to. What is ancient within us all can find expression. We wander through the archaeology of our own mind.

My critics have been numerous. It is wise to be your own critic. Subject what you think to the most thorough examination and you will not be afraid when others offer their opinion.

Do I have anything new to say to the world? Well, I think what I said throughout my life was revolutionary. No one is irreplaceable and if I had not come along, someone else might have done what I did. But imagine they didn't. What would the world be like? What would the world be like if there was no Shakespeare or Goethe, no Galileo no Copernicus, no Darwin?

It is not my place to return and pronounce upon the world. Instead, if you have questions, ask them of yourself. What do you think? If my ideas help you to think, then they are useful and be my guest subject them to the best criticism. In your observations, stay close to the facts in the field of your enquiry, use what instruments you can devise to measure the secrets of the human soul, use what instruments you can devise to measure how well you listen.

There are prisons that incarcerate people for their political views. There are creeds, lay and religious, that imprison the mind. I saw myself as part of a long tradition that championed freedom of the human spirit. It is not a freedom that is granted by edict or conferred by another. It is a freedom that each human being must find and choose for themselves. 'Know thyself,' said Socrates. The only way to possess that freedom is through self-knowledge. The unexamined life is not worth living because the human potential that can be released when a person knows and accepts themselves is immeasurable. The world needs people with that energy.

I turned a spotlight on many human intimacies, personal, emotional, sexual. I offered a language to enable people to speak about what was hidden. In much of life when we feel restricted, we are our own prison guards. We are afraid of what we think of ourselves. It is a great tragedy that a person spends a human life in fear of themselves, unable to find the words, unable to trust another human being to listen to them. Our mind can become like Bluebeard's castle full of secrets locked away. Over time, we forget what we have put in there; we live in unnamed fear.

*

With Freud departed, were I asked at this point to engage in an act of distillation, in response to a question, can you tell us in one sentence what you have said so far? Given that distillation is not reduction, is not a summary, but will point to the essence, the essential heartbeat, I answer in one word, listen.

Listen to your own words and thoughts. Listen to the way you receive the words and thoughts of others. Listen for the presence, or the absence of an in-between space, in your own mind and the mind of others. Listen for the transient, which the fretting mind can't see.

But I am now not just looking back but forward, and as I explore the scandal of sexual abuse of children in the Catholic church, I will note the wholesale absence of even the most rudimentary forms of listening.

4

Blessed Are Those Who Hunger and Thirst After Justice

Dawn breaks and the work of the graffiti artist is revealed. 'For all of life's complex questions there is a simple answer. And it's wrong.'

Why religious people who have dedicated their lives to God, and to the service of their fellow man, sexually abuse children is a complex question. Why fellow priests, bishops, cardinals and popes ignore and minimise the damage to the child's mind is a complex question. And why the Catholic church, here on earth to spread the Word of its Lord Jesus Christ – 'suffer little children to come unto me and forbid them not, for theirs is the kingdom of heaven' – engaged in legal trickery to withhold compensation and protect its material kingdom at all costs is a complex question.

The graffiti artist is right. And the simple answer is wrong.

As a psychoanalyst, I have an interest in the archaeology of the mind. I have an equal interest in the archaeology of the social – how a particular society in a particular country, at a particular time, came to be.

As an adult person can have influences within himself that affect his thought and behaviour, and of which he is unaware, so a society, a country, a particular group, can be shaped by events forgotten and obsolete. Ignorance of our individual history is a time bomb. Ignorance of our social history is a catastrophe waiting to happen.

Not all *ghaoths* and 'salamancas' are benign.

My exploration of child sexual abuse in the Catholic church begins in Ireland. I will relate aspects of Irish history that set the scene for the catastrophe that unfolded in the last half century. There have been many inquiries. I focus on one. The Murphy Commission investigated allegations against fifty-six priests in the Dublin archdiocese. Of those fifty-six, I examine two in detail.

I will also outline what understanding I have gained through my work as a psychoanalyst about the archaeology of the mind. If we agree we are dealing with complex questions, we will accept the need for complex answers.

The sexual abuse of children by religious people causes justifiable outrage. Such outrage needs to give way to thought. Before explaining how I think about this complex issue, it is necessary to explore some things that at first glance might seem unrelated.

A Catholic priest in Ireland had a privileged position. To appreciate that position, an understanding of some aspects of Irish history is necessary.

In chapters 4 to 8, I look at the issue of child sexual abuse by religious figures, in particular by priests in the Irish Catholic church. It is the church and country I know most about. The subject carries a warning such as appears before the viewing of a TV documentary or film that alerts to violence and explicit sexual content. A central principle of this chapter is the belief that if you want to understand someone properly, you have to acquaint yourself with their environment, with the context within which they live. You need to know that person's emotional and mental environment, the area within which they feel and think. If, therefore, we are interested in knowing what goes on in the mind of the child who is assaulted and used as a sexual object by a priest, you are required to consider what is going on in the mind of the perpetrator. This subject may be repellent and painful to examine, but if our moral indignation prevents us from exploring that mind, I think that we will have failed to fully appreciate the horror of what the child struggles with and the damage that is done to their capacity to think. We could say that child sexual abuse is a crime and leave it at that. But I am of the view that the disintegrated state of the perpetrator's mind is like a virus that can infect the child's mind. It is like a limpet mine that adheres to the mind of the child and can blow it up.

A common reaction to a story about how, for example, a priest raped an altar boy is to define him and the act as evil. 'Evil' is a useful word. It may describe the act; it does not explain it. If we remain in the zone of 'evil', claiming it is an explanation, we will fail the child.

But there is another and perhaps more profound reason why we must go beyond. I think the Catholic church has 'explained' sexual abuse to itself as evil. This has let the church off the psychological hook. By that I mean it has failed to pursue an understanding of the psychology involved. It takes refuge, not just behind canon law, but more perversely behind theology.

In 2011 in the Irish parliament (the Dail) in Dublin, the prime minister (the taoiseach) Enda Kenny delivered a scathing denunciation of the Catholic church. The Cloyne Report revealed that the Holy See had attempted to frustrate an inquiry into the rape and torture of Irish children by clergy. Cloyne is a diocese that covers parts of County Cork in Ireland's south-west. The Vatican had interfered in a sovereign democratic nation and the crimes of priests downplayed to protect the reputation of the church. Pope Benedict's reaction to the Cloyne Report, the Taoiseach said, was 'to parse and analyse it with the gimlet eye of a canon lawyer'. The sexual abuse of children by priests in the Catholic church is one of the issues this book deals with. That an Irish prime minister could speak like that was an extraordinary event. A brief look at Irish history will show how extraordinary it was and will provide a context to explore the abuse of children by priests.

Until 1970, Catholics in Ireland were forbidden by the Catholic church to study at Trinity College Dublin, a Protestant university. Attending without a dispensation from the bishop of the diocese in which you lived risked excommunication. And in the same year the university authorities for the first time permitted a Catholic chaplain to operate within its confines.

In a radio broadcast on St Patrick's Day 1943, the then taoiseach (and future president) Eamon de Valera spoke of his vision of Ireland.

The Ireland that we dreamed of would be the home of a people who valued material wealth only as a basis for right living, of a people who, satisfied with frugal comfort, devoted their leisure to the things of the spirit…a land whose countryside would be bright with cosy homesteads, whose fields and villages would be joyous with the sounds of industry, with the romping of sturdy children, the contest of athletic youths and the laughter of happy maidens… a people living the life that God desires that men should live.

Going on a school excursion to Trinity College in the 1960s to see The Book of Kells had an attendant warning: to walk within those walls was to walk in the shadow of evil.

In 1922, attached to Britain for hundreds of years, Ireland detached itself and proceeded to fragment into civil war. After a year of killing, the death of a youthful leader by a sniper's bullet on a quiet country road shocked the nation. The killing stopped. How was life to go on? Into the space, the Catholic church stepped. Catholic doctrine was enshrined in the constitution. Religious orders ran schools, hospitals and social services. Books were banned; writers critical of church power exiled. By 1949, when Ireland officially became a republic, the religious and the secular were almost one, the shaft of light between them dim, often impossible to detect.

In the 1950s, rural Ireland had changed little since the 1830s. A new machine, the reaper and binder, appeared in the fields at harvest time and mowing bars felled the meadows, but in the barns and outhouses the recently discarded scythes and sickles hung on the walls and the vision of rows of women gathering and binding sheaves was still fresh in memory.

In 1829 at Westminster, the British parliament had passed the Catholic Emancipation Act. It permitted freedom of religion for Catholics. This change led to the construction of churches and schools all over Ireland. In many rural areas, enclosures were created with a church, a churchyard and a two-roomed, two-teacher primary school: a symbol of freedom, a promise of learning, a place to think.

When he set up the Second Vatican Council in 1962, Pope John

XXIII said it was meant to throw open the windows of the church and allow fresh air inside. In the mind of J.C. McQuaid (who was archbishop of Dublin when I grew up), however, the windows remained resolutely shut. On his return from the council, he gave a sermon at the Pro-cathedral in Dublin and said, 'no change will worry the tranquillity of your Christian lives'.

Having walked into obedience early in life, huge sections of the Irish people found it difficult to think for themselves and were very conflicted when anyone openly criticised the church. This discomfort with criticism was shown on Telefis Eireann's *The Late Late Show* in 1966. Trinity College student Brian Trevaskis appeared on the show and called the newly opened Galway Cathedral a 'ghastly monstrosity'. He accused the Bishop of Galway Michael Brown of 'extortion' over the manner in which funds were raised. He called the bishop a 'moron'. Trevaskis had spent part of his childhood in an orphanage and questioned this spending when there was so much poverty in the country. When building began in 1958 on what was to become the last great stone cathedral to be built in Europe, one-sixth of Ireland's population had to emigrate to find work. It took seven years to build and the opening ceremony illustrated how that faint light separating church and state was extinguished. At the ceremony, the Irish president Eamon de Valera lit the sanctuary candle and Cardinal Cushing from Boston delivered a sermon. I remember seeing Brian Trevaskis on *The Late Late Show* and the controversy that dominated the news during the week that followed. Pressure was put on Trevaskis to return the following week to apologise.

When church and state are intertwined, confusion is created. Hypocrisy and concealment of crimes flourish. In confusion no one can think straight. While J.C. McQuaid publicly reassured his flock – 'no change will worry the tranquillity of your Christian lives' – he connived with Police Commissioner Costigan to conceal child sexual abuse by priests. When one priest, Father James McNamee, who abused children for decades, denied his crimes, McQuaid believed him and said, 'as he is a worthy priest, I agree that we could not refuse to accept his word'.

*

There are twenty-six dioceses in Ireland and there have been a number of inquiries into sexual abuse by priests. The area of Ireland I focus on is the Dublin diocese, which is one of the largest in Ireland and covers the county and city of Dublin but also parts of five other counties. The Murphy Commission was set up to investigate sexual abuse by priests in the Dublin archdiocese. It investigated abuse from the 1960s onwards. To facilitate clarity concerning names and dates, I add that during the period under examination there were a number of Dublin archbishops, McQuaid (1940–1972), Ryan (1972–1984), McNamara (1984–1987) and Connell (1988–2004). The present archbishop, Diarmuid Martin, succeeded Bishop Connell in 2004.

The Murphy report was produced in November 2009. In the following chapters, I draw heavily on that report. Having already given the Irish names for parliament and PM, I will add that in Ireland a policeman is called a garda. The plural is gardai. The police service is called the Gardai Siochana.

*

I begin with the case of a Dublin priest Father Noel Reynolds. Noel Reynolds was born in 1933. He had entered the Dublin diocesan seminary Clonliffe College in 1952 and was ordained a priest in 1959. He spent periods as a chaplain to a number of girls' schools before being appointed in 1969 as a curate to Kilmore Road parish in Dublin. In 1978, he was moved to East Wall parish, also in Dublin, until August 1983, when he was transferred to the diocese of Tuam in western Ireland and stationed on an island off the coast. He returned to the Dublin diocese in 1984 and spent time as a curate in two parishes, Bonnybrook and Saggart, before being made parish priest at Glendalough in County Wicklow in 1992. It was there in 1994 that concerns were expressed to a neighbouring curate about his behaviour with young children. These matters were reported to the chancellor of the Dublin archdiocese, Monsignor Stenson, in September 1995.

A month later, in October 1995, Archbishop Connell issued a decree initiating a preliminary investigation into complaints from Glendalough under canon 1717 of the code of canon law. Monsignor Stenson was appointed as delegate. Four months later, February 1996, Monsignor Stenson met the school principal to receive details of the complaint. And thirteen months later, in March 1996, Monsignor Stenson met Reynolds. In April, the monsignor reported to the diocesan panel. The panel concluded there was no firm evidence that any incidents of child sexual abuse had taken place. It accepted that some 'inappropriate behaviour' had occurred. The panel recommended assessment by Dr Patrick Walsh at the Granada Institute. More than two years had elapsed since the original complaint and Reynolds was still parish priest at Glendalough.

The Granada Institute was opened in 1994, in Shankill, County Dublin on the recommendation of the Irish Bishops Conference held in the same year. It was administered by the St John of God Brothers.

Dr Walsh concluded that Reynolds exhibited

> considerable confusion in his relationships with children. He has confused his own needs as a child with their needs and consequently has failed to maintain appropriate adult-child boundaries. In addition, he has used inappropriate language in his classes and interaction with children.

Dr Walsh recommended that a priest support person be put in place for him. This was not done until July 1998. Meanwhile, Reynolds was appointed chaplain to the National Rehabilitation Hospital, Rochestown Avnue, Dun Laoghaire, in July 1997 by Archbishop Connell. The Granada Institute was not informed of this appointment.

The National Rehabilitation Hospital had a children's ward and a school. The hospital authorities were not informed of Reynolds's history. When the hospital management discovered it in 2002, they complained to Cardinal Connell. He replied in the following terms:

> No explanation of mine could justify the fact that the National Rehabilitation Hospital was not informed of this background at the time of Father Reynolds' appointment as chaplain. I acknowledge that this was a serious error, although made without realisation of the risk involved.

When the history, the nature and the extent of Reynolds's abuse of children emerged, it revealed a pattern that is familiar. Decades of abuse in many places and multiple victims; colleagues who turned a blind eye; a church establishment totally incapable of listening, and parts of the establishment that actively promoted a policy of turning away and refusing to listen.

In February 1998, a woman spoke to the chancellor of the archdiocese, Monsignor Dolan, indicating that her daughter had been sexually abused by a priest some twenty years previously. She did not give the name of the priest nor was she asked for it. Monsignor Dolan told her that, as her daughter was now an adult, she would have to make the complaint herself. She was also told that if the complaint passed the threshold of suspicion, it would have to be reported to the gardaí. The mother expressed herself very pessimistic about the ability of her daughter to go to Archbishop's House.

The case was given to Auxiliary Bishop O'Mahony, who had a meeting with Dr Walsh and Reynolds in May 1998. Dr Walsh wrote to Bishop O'Mahony stating that he was of the firm view that Reynolds posed no threat to children. Six days after Dr Walsh wrote to Bishop O'Mahony, a social worker at a drug treatment centre contacted the chancellor, Monsignor Dolan, to tell him that a client had alleged that she had been abused by Father Reynolds when she was nine years old. She said she was particularly concerned because Reynolds was still the hospital chaplain. Archbishop Connell was notified of the social worker's allegations in late May 1998, and in July 1998 he released

Reynolds from his duties as chaplain to the National Rehabilitation Hospital and nominated him as a beneficiary of the Diocesan Clerical Fund. The hospital was not informed of the reasons for Reynolds's removal and assumed it was due to his poor health. By this time, Father Paddy Gleeson had been appointed assistant delegate and was now handling the matter on behalf of the archdiocese. Reynolds was medically examined and it was noted that, in addition to his cardiac problems, he suffered from the initial stages of diabetes and Parkinson's disease and that he should not live alone. He had been living with his sister and later moved in with his stepmother. In January 1999, a place was found for him in a nursing home.

In June 1999, Father Gleeson contacted the gardaí at the sexual assault unit at Harcourt Street and informed them that the archdiocese had received complaints of sexual abuse by Reynolds while he was attached to the parish of Kilmore West in the late 1970s.

A newspaper in August 1999 reported that the gardaí had launched a major investigation into rape claims by two sisters against an elderly priest. It also alleged that the priest had used a crucifix in what was described as a sick sex assault. The priest was not named. In October 1999, the gardaí received a complaint from another woman alleging that she had been sexually abused by Reynolds while he was a curate in Kilmore West in the 1970s. She alleged that, as she was preparing for her communion, he sat her on his knee and put his hands into her pants and put his finger into her vagina. This had happened on five separate occasions before she made her first communion. Reynolds was arrested in October 1999 for the offence of raping one of the two sisters referred to above between the years 1971 and 1979.

When interviewed, Reynolds admitted widespread abuse. He admitted abusing one of the sisters when she was eleven and the other when she was six years old and putting his finger into their vaginas when they were in bed in their own home. He told the gardaí that he was sexually attracted to young girls and that they were not the only two victims in Kilmore. He could remember about twenty girls in total; there were others in East Wall and in the diocese of Tuam. He admitted inserting a crucifix into one girl's vagina and back passage. He said he had admitted to their mother that he had abused her daughters. He said he offered their mother £30,000 in compensation but that she did not accept it. Not only did he admit the abuse of the two sisters and several others in many other parishes, but he also offered as evidence to the gardaí the crucifix with which he had said he had abused one of the complainants.

The gardaí became aware of another twelve complainants. The incidents ranged from fondling of genitals to touching around the leg area, digital penetration, anal rape, attempted sexual intercourse, oral sex, actual sexual intercourse and inviting the children to fondle his penis. In many cases, the abuse continued for between two and seven years. In total, nine females and six males came forward and said they were abused by Reynolds. They were aged between six years and eleven years at the time of the abuse. He admitted to many more cases of abuse, at least twenty in Kilmore alone.

When Reynolds spoke about himself, the following was revealed. His mother died when he was very young and at eight he was sent to a boarding school run by the Holy Ghost religious order, where he was extremely lonely. He applied to train as a priest with the Holy Ghost Order but they deemed him unsuitable. He entered the Dublin diocesan training centre, Clonliffe College, on the personal recommendation of Archbishop McQuaid. During the course of his curacy at Kilmore Road, when he had already begun abusing children, he wrote a very unusual seven-page letter to Archbishop Ryan about the deep unrest that was permeating his life. He stated that 'a feeling of unrest has been continually with me for the past six months or so. I am upset by the quality of my life... Would it be possible to live with the poor? To live with a family...'. Nothing was done about this.

In March 1996, Monsignor Stenson, in his capacity as delegate, met Reynolds. The following are extracts from what Reynolds said in that meeting.

It was my own folly rather than maliciousness... If I'd been assessed before going into Clonliffe I would have been [seen as] a repressed person and in need of affection. My mother died at 4. [I was] longing for love. In 1959 in Dundrum Tech I freaked giving children a class on sex instruction. I was always trying to disassociate the idea of dirt from sex... I believe loneliness as a child has been a huge factor. I would admit that my sexual orientation is towards children. Children would arouse me sexually. My orientation to children has caused me much pain... I have a funny feeling that I never had an adolescence. At 63 my judgement in these areas of children has been foolish. I think I can control it. It was a habit. I think I can avoid bad behaviour any more –imprudent – folly. I will go for any help that is required. I thought of joining a monastery as a secluded monk but admitted, I'm still journeying myself. But there is an element of letting me be 70 million miles away from all this...the school, allegations etc.'

When, in 1983, Reynolds sought a transfer from Dublin to Tuam to work on an island off the west coast of Ireland, he told the archbishop that he wanted to 'be more in tune with the people...to give away everything (or as much as possible) and separate myself from life in Dublin where there are far too many distractions'.

When Archbishop Ryan wrote to Archbishop Cunnane of Tuam he said, 'Father Noel Reynolds is a dedicated and devoted priest and will give good service to the Islanders.' He also told Reynolds, 'I am informing him of your identity, which so far has been carefully concealed.'

While in East Wall parish (from 1978 until August 1983), the parish priest went into Reynolds's bedroom one evening to turn off the light and noted a female lying asleep in his bed. He considered she was around thirty years old. According to his statement to gardaí in July 1997, he said he was shocked by the discovery but that he did not speak to Reynolds or anybody else about the matter. It is highly unlikely that the female in Reynolds's bed was a thirty-year-old woman given his admitted propensity for young children. Later, in his garda interviews, Reynolds admitted to abusing a female teenager over a period of two days while he was in East Wall and the evidence strongly suggests that it was that teenager who was in Reynolds's bed.

*

Father Paul McGennis was born in 1931 and ordained in 1957. He was chaplain to Our Lady's Hospital for Sick Children from 1958 to 1960. He subsequently held a number of appointments in the archdiocese. His faculties were withdrawn in 1997. In that same year, he was convicted of indecent assault against two girls and served a term of nine months' imprisonment.

In August 1960, Archbishop McQuaid was informed that a security officer at a photographic film company in the UK had referred to Scotland Yard colour film sent to them for developing by McGennis. Scotland Yard referred the matter to the commissioner of the gardaí. There is no evidence of any garda investigation. However, Garda Commissioner Costigan met Archbishop McQuaid and, according to Archbishop McQuaid's note of the meeting, told him that the photographic company had 'handed to Scotland Yard a colour film with label Rev. [McGennis], Children's Hospital, Crumlin, Dublin, of which 26 transparencies were of the private parts of two small girls, aged 10 or 11 years'. The garda commissioner asked Archbishop McQuaid to take over the case because a priest was in question and the gardaí 'could prove nothing'. No attempt seems to have been made to establish who the two girls in the photographs were. The commission considers that it was totally inappropriate and a breach of duty for the garda commissioner to simply hand over the complaint to Archbishop McQuaid without carrying out any thorough investigation.

Archbishop McQuaid immediately referred the case to his auxiliary bishop, Bishop Dunne. Bishop Dunne expressed the view that a crime of child sexual abuse had been committed. The next day, Archbishop McQuaid met McGennis, who admitted photographing the children in sexual postures alone and in groups. These photographs were taken in Crumlin hospital. The archbishop's record is as follows:

> The children were playing about, lifting their clothes. He rebuked them. Seeing this was a chance of discovering what the genitals

were like, he pretended there was no film in the camera he was carrying and photographed them in sexual postures, alone and seated together, chiefly in a way or posture that opened up the parts. He declared that he had done so, as one would take an art photo., seeing no grave sin at all and suffering no physical disturbance in himself. He was puzzled, though he had seen line drawings, as to structure and functions of females. In questioning, I discovered that he had been reared with brothers, had never moved about socially with girls and tended to avoid them as in the hospital with the nurses. I suggested I would get [a doctor] a good Catholic to instruct him and thus end his wonderment.' Archbishop McQuaid also recorded: 'I felt that he clearly understood the nature of the sinful act involved and to send him on retreat would defame him.'

The Murphy Commission stated that this case was very badly handled by Archbishop McQuaid. McQuaid's conclusion that McGennis's actions arose merely from a 'wonderment' about the female anatomy was risible. The commission considered there are two possible explanations for such a view. Either Archbishop McQuaid could not deal with the fact that a priest who was in a privileged position of chaplain to a children's hospital fundamentally abused that position and sexually exploited vulnerable young children awaiting treatment, or he needed an explanation which would deal with Bishop Dunne's justifiable concern and which would also justify not reporting the matter to Rome. The commission considered that the second explanation the most likely.

In 1922, Pope Pius XI wrote a confidential memo about crimes of solicitation (*Crimen sollicitationis*). The memo required all investigations by the church of clerical abuse (homosexuality, bestiality, child abuse, soliciting sex in the confessional) to be carried out in strict confidentiality and dealt with inside the church. The penalty for breaching confidentiality, including reporting to the police, was automatic excommunication.

This case of McGennis had a special significance because it was one of the earliest in the commission's remit. The apparent cancellation by Archbishop McQuaid of his original plan to pursue the priest through the procedures of canon law was a disaster. It established a pattern of not holding abusers accountable which lasted for decades. Firmer treatment of this priest might have avoided much abuse in the future. The archbishop and Bishop Dunne had no doubt that a serious crime had been committed but avoided taking any action, as that would have entailed Rome becoming involved in the case. The archbishop appointed Bishop Dunne to investigate the case and, in the commission's view, promptly undermined him in his position.

In the commission's view, Archbishop McQuaid's actions fell very short of what should have been done. Given that he was fully aware of the 1922 instruction, there was no justification for his failure to set up a proper canonical process to deal with the matter. In fact, he deliberately manipulated the situation in a manner that did not involve him reporting the matter to Rome. No attempt was made to put protocols in place for chaplains throughout the many hospitals in which they were working in the Dublin archdiocese and no attempt was made to monitor McGennis in other placements.

Marie Collins was one of a number of young people sexually abused by McGennis at Crumlin hospital. She approached her local curate, Father Eddie Griffin, in November 1985 when she was thirty-eight, and told him about her abuse. She had been sexually abused and photographed by McGennis in Crumlin hospital in 1960 when she was aged thirteen. The curate indicated to her that he did not want to know the name of her abuser as he would have to do something about it. In a statement he made to the gardaí in 2004, he said,

> I didn't want to know the name of the priest. If she told me the name of the priest, I had to do something about it… I told her not to feel any guilt about what had happened and that the priest had done wrong… When she didn't tell me his name, I wondered why she was there and thought she might be feeling guilty and I told her I could do away with her guilt by giving her absolution.

How Griffin could have formed a view that she might be feeling guilty and in need of absolution when, in fact, she was disclosing abuse was difficult for the commission to understand. His assertion that, as priests, they had been advised in college not to seek the names of priests against whom allegations were being made in a spiritual or counselling context was a great concern to the commission. Such an attitude would explain in large measure the many appalling deficiencies in the church's handling of complaints of child sexual abuse over the years.

The Murphy Commission also said Archbishop Connell and Monsignor Stenson, in their dealings with Mrs Collins, were not initially open with her. They failed to tell her that there was a pre-existing complaint and other concerns. Like many of those abused, she was thus isolated and left to believe that she was the only one who had complained.

Monsignor Stenson believed that Mrs Collins had been abused by McGennis, but felt precluded by canon law from involving the police. He left Mrs Collins in a difficult situation by telling her that the priest had admitted her abuse and then not acknowledging that to the gardaí.

In 1996, the Dublin archdiocese produced a 'Framework Document' that outlined how sexual abuse cases should be handled, but then continued to ignore its own guidelines. The framework document stated,

> If the bishop or religious superior is satisfied that child sexual abuse has occurred, appropriate steps should be taken to ensure that the accused priest or religious does not remain in any pastoral appointment which affords access to children.

But McGennis remained in the parish dressed as a priest and taking part in parish functions.

The Murphy Commission concluded that everything that Mrs Collins managed to extract from the archdiocese over the years in relation to the handling of child sexual abuse was given grudgingly and always after a struggle. Mrs Collins now believes, on the basis of bitter experience, that her church cannot be trusted to deal properly with complaints of child sexual abuse and that legal measures are required to ensure compliance by the church with proper standards of child protection. The commission also notes that, notwithstanding her own reservations in the matter, there is no doubt that Mrs Collins, in her brave and often lonely campaign to show the archdiocese how it had erred in its handling of child sexual abuse cases, was instrumental in changing the archdiocese's understanding and handling of these cases and of bringing about a far greater atmosphere of openness about the incidence and handling of child sexual abuse.

5

Suffer Little Children to Come to Me

I turn now to outline the understanding I have gained through my work as a psychoanalyst about the archaeology of the mind of the child. It is relevant to add here that I was a social worker for seventeen years. I worked as a field social worker in child protection and as a psychiatric social worker in a multidisciplinary child guidance clinic. During those years, I studied at the Tavistock Clinic in London.

The best learning takes place in the company of colleagues from other professions who do similar work. Beyond your immediate circle, books, journals and conferences provide access to the experience and thought of people all over the world. Apart from my direct clinical experience, many psychotherapist, psychiatrists and psychologists have consulted with me about people who sought help following sexual abuse as children. Out of all that, I have created two children I call Patrick and Brigit. Brigit was abused by her father and Patrick was abused by a priest. But these are not actual children. Confidentiality requires the protection of information about cases that are not in the public realm. But Brigit and Patrick are very real. I know of many 'Brigits' and 'Patricks'. Having created them, I find they match many actual case histories. Doing it this way, protects the privacy of actual people. And we mustn't lose sight of the main game. However we achieve it, better understanding leads to improved thought and to an increased capacity to listen.

*

Brigit lay in her bed and stared at a family photograph on the bedside table. In her new school uniform, she stood between her mother and father. They all smiled at the camera. In the half-light, Brigit examined her father's face. Since she started school, he'd spent a lot of time away in the army. When he came home last year, he was changed. He seldom spoke to her; he often left the house in the evenings returning when it was dark. Last week he forgot her seventh birthday.

She looked in the photo for the father she once knew; who came to her bedroom every night to read a story, who when she was fretful held her hand and sang her softly to sleep.

Since her brother was born six months ago, her mother had looked sad. When she smiled, she made the smile come and whenever the baby slept, she slept too.

Brigit was on the edge of sleep when the door of the house opened and closed. She heard someone enter her room. Her father got into her bed. He took hold of her hand, placed it on his penis and masturbated.

If while driving a car someone hits you side on, at the moment of impact, your body goes rigid and your mind blanks.

Brigit's body went rigid and her mind blanked.

*

Patrick was seven in 1966. It was the day of his first communion. The sacred wafer, the body of Christ, was placed on his tongue. Photographed in his new suit, with his hands joined, he was the recipient of many half-crowns that jingled in his pocket. Filled with a sense of sanctification, he whispered to his mother that he wanted to become a priest. He'd had a dream the night before. It was his ordination. His hands were anointed with the sacred oils. He celebrated his first mass and gave her his first blessing.

In the week that followed, there was much talk about a student who called a bishop a moron. Patrick's father angrily read from the paper. The student's name was Trevaskis. His father said he was a right heathen. Patrick was horrified at what the student had said and that night said extra prayers and promised God that he would always stand up for His church.

A new priest, Father Kelly, arrived in the parish and was visiting all the families who had a child who had made their first communion. Father Kelly had been stationed in England and had done great work with the homeless. Kelly was treated with great reverence when he came to Patrick's house for tea. Over the following months, Father Kelly became a frequent visitor. Patrick struggled with his reading and writing and Father Kelly provided some excellent tuition. Patrick's parents were delighted and there was even more reason to sing the priest's praise.

One day when Father Kelly visited, Patrick was ill in bed. His mother told the priest that she was not sure if he was really unwell or worried again about his schoolwork. Father Kelly offered to go and see Patrick in his bedroom. The priest worked wonders again and it wasn't long before he was regularly going with Patrick to his bedroom – it was the only quiet part of the house – to help him with his schoolwork. His five siblings were jealous but Patrick, who by now was often spoken about as having a vocation, felt very special.

And Father Kelly voiced his own views to Patrick that he was a very special boy. One day, the priest's hand, which from time to time had guided Patrick's hand across the page if his writing veered off line, took the boy's hand and placed it on his penis. As the priest masturbated with his own and Patrick's hand cupped together, he told Patrick this was their secret. Patrick made to cry out. Father Kelly whispered in Patrick's ear that there was nothing wrong. He said God gave special privileges to priests and to boys who had a vocation. I've prayed to God for you and me, he told the boy, and God told me it was all right to do this together.

Patrick knew priests didn't marry or have children. He was often told that a priest was so close to Christ there was no need for a family and that celibacy was a great virtue. He also heard in a sermon that the church was the bride of Christ and that the union between a married couple can't ever end in divorce, because it represented the union between God and the church, which would never be broken. When he had told his mother that he wanted to be a priest, she gave him a decorated prayer card. It was a prayer for purity, for the grace to remain a virgin. Every night, Patrick had gone down on his knees, asked God for grace and promised to be pure.

But the night after Father Kelly had touched his private parts, when Patrick knelt at his bed and tried to pray, he couldn't. The quietness he'd loved was gone; instead of stillness, his mind raced. Something in him forbade anger. It was the fourth of the seven deadly sins. To admit to anger with a priest would make him a right heathen.

Patrick grew frantic. God, who had been so close, was far away. The next time Father Kelly went to the boy's bedroom, the priest's hands moved to Patrick's bottom. And when the priest pushed his penis into Patrick's anus, the boys mind split into many pieces. The priest, whose hands had been anointed with the sacred oils, had taken the boy to hell.

*

When I learn about events such as I have described, I am, like every other person, shocked and feel within myself the pain and suffering of the child. Abhorrence and the accompanying moral indignation often define the debate that follows such revelations. In many instances, the listeners are themselves in some way traumatised and unable to progress to the next stage. Enda Kenny's 2011 speech in the Dail was one spoken not only from abhorrence, but he had taken care to think about the situation.

I will outline how I think about child sexual abuse. There are many features to such abuse but I will continue to place emphasis on what goes on in the mind of the child.

When the seven-year-old Brigit becomes fourteen, twenty-one, twenty-eight, her mind may still be blank. And Patrick may pass through the same signposts of his life with his mind split into many pieces. You might have difficulty seeing this from the outside. To go inside, to explore the inner world a map is needed. Our compassion and empathy for a suffering person is essential but not sufficient. If I feel distress listening to instances of child sexual abuse and assault, I am acting like any other person. But if I am to listen as a psychoanalyst, I need help. I need clarity of thought. There are two people whom I find particularly helpful. One is Hans Loewald and the other Ronald Fairbairn. Both were psychiatrists and psychoanalysts and had an interest in philosophy (and were gifted communicators), and each trusted a spark of originality within their minds that enabled them to shine a light on obscure mental activity.

Their ideas are now interwoven in my mind, so what follows is the product of that interweaving. I have studied and used their thought extensively, so instead of quoting them I will try to convey their understanding in my own words. I begin with how we perceive what is normal, good development.

Humans are social animals and while we instinctually preserve our own life and protect ourselves from whatever threatens that life, we also survive and thrive as part of a community of others; our family, our social group, our tribe, our nation. We need to grow and develop and adapt. In our dependent state as child, we need food, drink, shelter and protection from danger. We need to be loved and learn to love. That is the emotional foundation on which we are built. We slowly learn that we are separate from others, that 'I' is other than 'you'. We move not from dependency to independency but from immature dependency to mature dependency, to become a competent and responsible adult requires that we relinquish an immature dependence on our parents. To learn to be adult, we must acquire their power and become our own authority. We need to be able to 'say' to them, 'I don't need you in that way any more, I can do it without you.' This is a developmental necessity. But we also include their authority within us. We stand beside our parents and think as adults with them. Our identity is now both theirs and ours.

Hans Loewald writes of the 'family bond' which binds our very identity. We become who we are in and through the identifications with our mother, father and siblings. These bonds are sacred in the sense that they are primary; they are above and beyond all else in the sense that they are the foundations of our personal identity; and they are the boundaries that contain and define our personhood, the very shape and structure of our psychic reality and stability.

To subsequently take a person whose self has been so constructed and make them an object of adult genital sexuality is to violate, exploit, defy and overturn that primary identification. Incest involves the destruction of these early and primary identifications. In its secrecy, it also contains the exclusion and destruction of the others in the family and a denial of generational differences. Loewald named it 'an intermediate ambiguous state'. The anxiety that is then felt reflects the danger and uncertainty of living now in this secret intermediate state, the creation of which has required the ruination of what has gone before. The extreme nature of the anxiety (and its subsequent need for negation) is related to the fear of one's identity being lost, shattered and fragmented. It is against this background that the word 'perversion' assumes its meaning. In child sexual abuse and incest, the perpetrator perverts the course of the child's normal healthy development. The reality of the child's particular age and her specific stage of physical, emotional and cognitive development are denied.

In the film *Sophie's Choice,* a mother with two children has to decide which one will be sent to a children's labour camp and which will go to the gas chamber at Auschwitz. A child who is being sexually abused by its parent is psychically placed in a similar impossible dilemma. A psychological trade-off takes place. This is not so much a choice as a necessity. There is nothing as humanly terrifying as the threat of mental disintegration. It is the psychic equivalent of personal annihilation. Having taken in the goodness of life from the parent, having been constructed by the parent, the child has to hold on to a belief that the parent is good. As the parent has been in a position of not just bodily but psychologically creating the child, the child cannot just psychologically ignore the adult. The child takes into itself the badness and some part of the child's ego or self aligns with it. The principle is that having some control – albeit at a cost – is better than doing nothing. In fact, doing nothing is not an option: there is an internal identification with the one who is initiating the abuse. In the interests of survival and by way of providing some protection in the event of a reoccurrence, the child, descriptively speaking, tries 'to get its mind around' the workings of the abuser's mind.

In *Sophie's Choice*, the mother, Sophie, eventually commits suicide. Her action with her children was external to herself, but eventually she could no longer live with what she had done. The action of the abused child is internal to itself. It has sacrificed part of its self and taken badness inside in order to survive. This understanding can explain why the sexually abused child may later take their own life. It can also explain why those who go on living carry within themselves a sense of badness.

Let me explain. The parent forced to send one child to death to save the other is in one of the worst human dilemmas imaginable. A child who is sexually abused has to do a trade like Sophie. That trade culminates in a 'suicide'. If we establish/accept the above and come at it again, this time with Loewald's help, we find that the sexually abused child had two ways to commit 'suicide'. To sever the primary sacred bonds to a parent is one form of suicide. To extinguish a good part of yourself is another form of suicide.

You try to salvage something from the wreckage of an impossible situation. A fox with its leg in a trap will chew off its limb; some lizards and crabs simply cast off a part of their body to effect escape, a process in zoology called autotomy. Certain trees in a drought amputate their own branches. With humans, the primary identification with the parent must be preserved and so a part of the self must be sacrificed and amputated.

This combination of conditions, in my opinion, helps to understand the sense of guilt and responsibility, shame and badness that can persist through the child's and adult's life. And if we take this line of thought to its logical conclusion, by a perverse/cruel twist of fate, he/she is 'responsible'. They did amputate. That some never lead a productive (emotional) life can be explained by being stranded midway between two forms of suicide. They are in Loewald's 'intermediate ambiguous state' and are so taken up with the challenges and the dangers of that state that there is little to give others, few opportunities to love the world.

Looking at the internal 'worlds' of Brigit and Patrick, we can see many similarities. There are parallels between Brigit and her father and Patrick and Father John and many echoes we can listen out for: how the priest is in loco parentis; how the disintegration in the father's mind is replicated in the priest's mind; how exploring the mind of the child abused by the parent helps us to look into the mind of the child abused by the priest; how the madness in the mind of the priest and the parent is negated; how the child's mind becomes the receptacle, the place where the madness, the splitting, is projected.

*

At the conclusion of its report on Noel Reynolds, the Murphy Commission stated that the case was extremely badly handled by the archdiocese. Numerous indications of serious abuse and of admissions by Reynolds were ignored. It seemed to the commission that, had the two women themselves not complained to the gardaí, the archdiocese would have been quite happy to ignore the fact that any abuse had taken place.

The church's mindset or its mentality was elsewhere. By church, I refer not only to the hierarchy but also the individual priests that it trained. The catastrophic failure to protect children can be traced to the policy established by Pope Pius XI in 1922 when crimes became secrets to be held within the church and not reported to the secular authorities. The secrecy policy of the Vatican found its way down to the parish level. As already mentioned, when they were trained at Clonliffe College, priests were told not to ask the name of a priest about whom a complaint was made. In the words of one priest, 'We as priests had been advised while in college not to seek the name of priests that allegations were being made against.'

Within the mindset of not wanting to know and close it down at all costs, some priests engaged in a most perverse way of controlling abused children and adults. They used the practice and the notion of confession to heap guilt upon the abused. A girl who was anally raped by another priest tried to tell a priest in confession about it, but he refused to give her absolution. The shifting of guilt here is staggering. A girl who has been assaulted, and her family threatened, finds the courage to tell a trustworthy person. He can't accept the guilt of his fellow priest and pushes the guilt back on to the child.

Anyone who has learned the most rudimentary lesson of human psychology, indeed anyone with a scrap of common sense, knows the story of the scapegoat. All the sins and badness of the tribe are ritually put upon and into the goat that is then driven into the desert. This is a ritual cleansing of the psychologically primitive kind. Here it is practised by the priest in the confessional.

You'd have to wonder if these priests ever read Matthew 19:14, where Jesus said, 'Suffer little children, and forbid them not, to come unto me: for of such is the kingdom of heaven.'

A policy of secrecy, like a virus, spread throughout the whole clerical class of the church. It created defensiveness. But in my view it did something worse than that: it fostered and made a virtue of ignorance; it damaged the capacity to think. It is rather an irony that in retreating from modernism and rationalism, which, especially at the beginning of the twentieth century, were perceived as great evils by the church, the church became irrational, lost its capacity to think.

Sometimes an organisation can make a change that is seen at the time as useful but some time latter it proves to have detrimental effects. In 1870, the pope was declared infallible when he spoke *ex cathedra*. It was at the time strictly defined and has only been used once, in 1950. But a detrimental side effect was an elevation of the position of the pope and increased authoritarianism in the church and many Catholics saw the pope as having absolute authority on many issues. Of relevance to the issue of clerical child sexual abuse, we can consider how within this organisation a priest who abuses children does so in the knowledge that the church treats his behaviour as above the secular law and the church will shield him from secular sanction.

For a child walking into obedience, the gimlet eye of the canon lawyers parsed and analysed sins. At seven, when a child made his or her first confession, they were deemed to have reached the age of reason and therefore capable of committing a mortal sin. Dying with one of those on your soul led to everlasting torment in hell. Hell was spoken about with the same sense of reality as the farm next door, and with the same inevitability as the Irish weather. Among the more serious sins was the sin of omission, the failure to do what was right, the neglect of your duty when the welfare of another depended on you. Within this sort of language and concept of sinning, the church has many sins of omission on its soul.

In the *Oxford English Dictionary*, the word 'mind' has an extensive entry. Mind refers to the faculty of memory; the action or state of thinking about something; the state of a person's thoughts and feelings; the mental or psychic faculty; the seat of awareness, thought, volition and feeling; cognitive and emotional phenomena and powers as constituting a controlling system. The word 'mind' is frequently attached to other words: mindset, have a mind, lose your mind, put in or out of mind et cetera. It is a word at the centre of so much within us as humans that it is impossible and undesirable to tie it down. In a way, this whole book wanders through what it is to have a mind and use it. Hopefully, by the end of the book, the picture will become clearer. I will proceed with the acceptance that we can agree that a church can have a mind. Some may prefer to substitute the word 'mindset'.

I explore where the church's mind was, and the various manifestations of that mind. In that mind, protecting its reputation was paramount. It used scapegoats, often the complaining parent, or the child, upon whom and into whom the guilt the church refused to own was deposited. It ignored the damage to the child's mind and life. In entering into the inner world of children, it neglected to educate itself and perversely embraced ignorance and a refusal to think. Its one-size-fits-all notion of deviant behaviour by priests disabled it and left it unable to discriminate between psychopathic behaviour and the desperately lonely.

6

Blinded by the Light

When Brian Trevaskis returned to *The Late Late Show*, those who expected an apology were quickly disappointed. He continued his criticism of Bishop Michael Brown and extended it to the larger church and to the state. He described how women who had children outside marriage were outcasts. He said Ireland was not a Christian country. When asked if the bishop knew the meaning of the word 'moron', he replied suggesting the bishop did not know the meaning of the word 'Christian'.

Trevaskis's criticism of the state focused on the way the 1916 Easter rebellion was commemorated. Ireland at the time was in the grip of celebrating fifty years since the rebellion. I remember the occasion well. The leaders of the rebellion, especially Patrick Pearse, were spoken of with great reverence. In 1966, a special ten-shilling coin was struck and I acquired one, which I held on to for many years but in my various moves in and beyond Ireland somewhere was left behind. The coin was the first to contain the features of a political figure. Pearse in profile was on one side. On the other the mythical Irish hero Cu Chulainn.

In 1916, Patrick Pearse was declared, by those who followed him, to be the president of the provisional government of Ireland. After six days, the rebellion was crushed by the British forces (Ireland then was a part of the United Kingdom) and Pearse was the first of fifteen leaders to be executed.

We grew up with stories of this saintly figure, a poet and schoolmaster, a Gaelic speaker who had sacrificed himself for Ireland. While secular nationalism lifted him to hero status, the church played its part in elevating him to the position of saint and martyr. Here, Galway cathedral and Bishop Brown come back into the story. The bishop arranged for a mosaic to be inserted into the wall of the side chapel. The mosaic has three figures. In the centre, a resurrected Jesus: on one side the assassinated US President John Fitzgerald Kennedy (who was a Catholic); on the other side Patrick Pearse. Pearse and Kennedy are praying. Pearse is in profile, the (only) image of him we all grew up with. He gazed into the distance as if within a vision.

In death, Pearse became a mythical figure. This figure was created by church and state. Where church and state fuse, where the boundaries between the two become blurred and overlap, I think there is need to create such mythical figures, to hold the two together, for the union to perpetuate itself. Certain people are good candidates for such exultation.

Pearse made himself into such a candidate. Before he became interested in politics, he was a zealous champion of all things Irish, especially the Irish language and set up a private school, St Enda's, in Dublin. All things Irish were idealised, good and wholesome; what was non-Irish was worthless. You were either with him or against him. He speaks for himself:

> If some of the old Masters had known rural Ireland, we should not have so many gross and merely earthly conceptions of the Madonna as we have.
>
> He [the Irish-speaking child] is the fairest thing that springs from the soil of Ireland – more beautiful than any flower, more graceful than any wild creature of the fields or the woods, purer than any monk or nun, wiser than any seer.
>
> Let us plainly tell the emigrant that he is a traitor to the Irish state.

Pearse's patriotism melded with his religious fanaticism. Those boys who attended his school were, in his eyes, not there simply to learn and preserve the Irish language, but to become soldiers for his cause. He melded religion and politics so much they became indistinguishable.

> We pursue her [England] like a sleuth-hound; we lie in wait for her and come upon her like a thief in the night; and some day we will overwhelm her with the wrath of God…It is not that we are apostles of hate. Who like us has carried Christ's word of charity about the earth? But the Christ that said 'My peace I leave you. My peace I give you', is the same Christ that said 'I bring you not peace, but a sword.' There can be no peace between right and wrong, between truth and falsehood, between justice and oppression, between freedom and tyranny. Between them is eternal war.

Pearse's elevation to mythical status began soon after he was executed and spread beyond Ireland. In Melbourne in 1920, Cardinal Mannix made a film about the Easter Rising in which the leaders who were executed were called heroes and martyrs. Mannix had been on the teaching staff at Maynooth seminary in Kildare and knew about Pearse and been the object of Pearse's criticism in his zeal to promote the Irish language. Pearse expected the church authorities to take a more active part in its revival.

Time and scholarship have removed Pearse from his exalted position and revealed him as a deeply flawed man. Since 1966, various people have looked at him head on. (He was pictured in profile because he had a disfiguring squint in his left eye.) He would visit places like the Aran Islands, where everyone spoke Irish, stay in their house, eat their food, wax lyrical about their blessed state, completely oblivious to their poverty. Considerations of the civilian collateral damage caused by his futile occupation of the GPO in Dublin would never have entered his head. Sixty rebels were killed in the 1916 insurrection. A hundred and thirty-two soldiers and police died. And three hundred civilians lost their lives.

In 1966, the full death count was never mentioned and no mention was ever made of Pearse's personal life (except perhaps a poem, called 'The Mother', he wrote to his mother before his death. In primary school, we had to learn it by heart. Its opening stanza still rattles around in my head.

> I do not grudge them Lord, I do not grudge
> My two strong sons I have seen go out
> To break their strength and die, they and a few
> In bloody protest for a glorious thing.

He wrote a different poem during his time as headmaster of St Enda's which also got no mention in 1966. It is called 'Little Lad of the Tricks'.

> Little lad of the tricks,
> Full well I know
> That you have been in mischief:
> Confess your fault truly.
>
> I forgive you, child
> Of the soft red mouth:
> I will not condemn anyone
> For a sin not understood.
>
> Raise your comely head
> Till I kiss your mouth:
> If either of us is the better of that
> I am the better of it.
>
> There is a fragrance in your kiss
> That I have not found yet
> In the kisses of women
> Or in the honey of their bodies.
>
> Lad of the grey eyes,
> That flush in thy cheek
> Would be white with dread of me
> Could you read my secrets.
>
> He who has my secrets
> Is not fit to touch you:

> Is not that a pitiful thing,
> Little lad of the tricks?

During a visit to a family in Aran, when the issue arose as to where he would sleep, Pearse asked to share the bed of the fourteen-year-old son. It is said he and the boy talked for an hour before falling asleep. The historian Ruth Dudley Edwards referred to Pearse's apparent sexual immaturity, while the historian Joost Augusteijn's view was

> Although it will not be possible to ascertain whether Patrick was a latent or active paedophile, beyond his tendency to kiss boys, it seems most probable that he was sexually inclined this way.

Pearse's poem 'The Mother' establishes his mother as the narrator in the poem. Later in the poem, we read,

> They shall be spoken of among their people
> The generations shall remember them
> And call them blessed;
> But I will speak their names to my own heart
> In the long nights.

But this is Pearse writing for himself, establishing himself as a martyr. The way he speaks resonates with the way the Gospels recount Jesus speaking to his mother from the cross. Which takes me back to the mosaic in Galway cathedral, and I could imagine that he would not be at all surprised to be in such company. He would consider it his rightful place. He might have guessed that when the political change he played his part in bringing about was embodied in a new Irish constitution, that document would begin with the following words:

> In the Name of the Most Holy Trinity, from Whom is all authority and to Whom, as our final end, all actions both of men and states must be referred, we, the people of Éire, humbly acknowledging all our obligations to our Divine Lord, Jesus Christ, Who sustained our fathers through centuries of trial…

When Patrick Pearse died his glorious death in 1916, a twenty-seven-year-old Ronald Fairbairn served in the British army in Palestine. Fairbairn had studied philosophy, theology and Greek. He had intended to be a lawyer, but the casualties of war and the suffering that persisted in the minds of traumatised soldiers caused him to change course. He returned to his native Edinburgh to medicine and became a psychiatrist. He read Freud and was impressed by his spirit of enquiry into the human mind. Unrestricted by dogma, Fairbairn pursued an independent line of investigation and, while becoming a psychoanalyst, presented his own ideas of the mind.

Fairbairn studied the divisions, the splits that can occur in the mind. He coined the term 'schizoid states' to describe those splits. The person with a schizoid mind makes a firm dividing line between love and hate, good and bad, holiness and evil. Such people have little or no empathy and avoid emotional contact with other people, except in very restricted and controlled circumstances. In some, intellectual values take the place of emotional values; ideas are loved and pursued with passion.

When he moved from studying the private individual to the political leader, Fairbairn said,

> when we find a really schizoid personality in love with some extreme political philosophy, the consequences become more serious, because the toll of victims may then run into millions. Such a personality, when he is in love with an intellectual system which he interprets rigidly and applies universally, has all the makings of a fanatic – which indeed is what he really is.

*

What Fairbairn described was much in evidence in Adolf Eichmann's case. When Eichmann was on trial for the crimes of the Third Reich, one of the judges asked him, 'Did you ever feel any conflict between your duty and your conscience?'

Eichmann: 'One could call it a state of being split. A conscious split state. Where one could flee from one side to the other.'

Judge: 'One's conscience was to be abandoned?'

Eichmann: 'You could say that.'

Judge: 'If there had been more civil courage, things could have been different?'

Eichmann: 'If civil courage had been hierarchically organised, then yes, absolutely.'

I do not compare Eichmann's actions with Pearse's. That would be absurd. But an examination of the extremes can allow clarity of thought about the less extreme. Pearse had splits in his mind. He could not think about the poor. Or the boys at St Edna's. He was a political fanatic. '[At St Enda's] it will be attempted to inculcate in them the desire to spend their lives working hard and jealously for their fatherland and, if it should be necessary, to die for it,' he said. Words that would have often been said in Eichmann's Germany! I would not wish to life in a country where the fanaticism Pearse espoused became the ruling order. It is called fascism. It is called totalitarianism.

I have highlighted Pearse because it is a good illustration of the fusion of church and state, which creates a situation where there is little or no space for examination and critical thought. I use a simple picture of a triangle. One side is the church; one the state. The third is a mutual agreement not to look too closely at the other. Everything will move along just fine! McQuaid and President Eamon de Valera epitomised this. Three years before he gave his 1943 St Patrick's Day radio broadcast (when he spoke of his vision of the Irish as a people 'satisfied with frugal comfort, devoted…to the things of the spirit…living the life that God desires that men should live'), McQuaid was appointed archbishop of Dublin. De Valera had petitioned the Vatican in the 1930s for this appointment and also for McQuaid to be made primate of all Ireland.

McQuaid died in 1973 and, when viewing his laid-out body, de Valera wept. De Valera's tears were observed and recorded. He himself was dead within the year and many tears were shed for him. How many children unprotected by McQuaid and unknown to a president committed to his blinkered view of life, in 1973, while being sexually assaulted by priests were weeping alone, and in silence?

*

I said earlier if we are interested in knowing what goes on in the mind of the child subjected to inappropriate sexual actions by a priest, we need to know what is going on in the mind of the perpetrator. In speaking about 'Brigit' and 'Patrick' and making use of Loewald and Fairbairn, I have attended to what goes on in part of the mind of the priest-perpetrator. We can't stop there. We must continue to explore the other aspects of the priest's 'mind'. An ordained, anointed priest has offered his mind to God, to allow God to be present within his community. The doctrine of the incarnation infused the practice of the sacraments. Through the priest's mind and his actions, God is embodied in everyday life.

Take this rule (a measuring device) and you will be better able to access the damage a priest can do to the mind and soul of a child whom he uses as a sexual object.

When the Murphy Commission reported in November 2009, the (then and present) Archbishop of Dublin Diarmuid Martin said the following:

> The hurt to a child through sexual abuse is horrific. Betrayal of trust is compounded by the theft of self-esteem. The horror can last a lifetime. Today, it must be unequivocally recalled that the Archdiocese of Dublin failed to recognise the theft of childhood which survivors endured and the diocese failed in its response to them when they had the courage to come forward, compounding the damage done to their innocence. For that no words of apology will ever be sufficient.

These sentiments are to be lauded, the acknowledgment of guilt and a failure to act, and the good intention to protect children in the future. It is a good place to start. But it is only a start.

When Patrick was instructed in preparation for his first confession, he would have been told about imperfect contrition and perfect contrition. When people who have been found to have done wrong apologise, the most common form of apology could be classified as imperfect contrition. An example which I shall call A: 'I did something bad. I should not have done it. I regret it. I'm disappointed because I have let myself down. If I have caused offence, I am sorry.'

An example, which I call B, of perfect contrition would go something like this: 'I see clearly the extent of the damage I have done to X. My action has caused them much pain and suffering. I am sorry. I will do everything I can to right the wrong I caused and to repair the damage. I hope my sincere apology and my actions from here on will enable them to recover.'

In A, the wrongdoer feels diminished. He experiences a sympathy for the other person but remains in a self-interested position. The damage to his own reputation is most important to him. B has empathy. Any damage to his own reputation or his view of himself is secondary to his concern for the other. His remorse is altruistic.

(Before continuing, it is worth nothing that the evidence of the Murphy Commission, and all the other inquiries in Ireland and beyond, suggests that the church was entrenched in a position of minus A!)

When Patrick received instruction about imperfect contrition and perfect contrition, the latter was presented as the most desirable. In the example of B above, the person has fully informed himself of the full extent of his wrongdoing. Has the church fully informed itself of the extent of its wrongdoing? I believe not. By looking at Patrick and using ideas from Hans Loewald and Ronald Fairbairn, it is possible to enter the deeper regions of the mind. Loewald used the word 'sacred' in a defined sense. The church makes extensive use of the word. If we extract the essence of Hans Loewald's ideas and the essence of Catholic teaching, there is much in common. Family bonds are very important. 'Give me the child to seven and I will give you the man.' The Holy Family, referring to Jesus, Mary and Joseph, have a significant place in Catholic piety. The church places God inside family bonds. The soul of each person is created by God, in His image and likeness. Eternal life with God is promised. Grace, essential for salvation, is God-given. The body is the temple of the Holy Spirit. The church is frequently referred to as 'Mother' church.

The ideas of Hans Loewald can be used to understand the church and its influence of a child's development. They allow us to probe into the issues that exists not just in the particular sexual abuse of a child by an individual priest, but the institutional reaction to that abuse and the inadequacy of the church's response to clerical child sexual abuse.

I drew attention above to the way Hans Loewald described how incest interfered with development. He wrote of the 'family bond' which binds our very identity. We become who we are in and through the identifications with our mother, father and siblings. These bonds are sacred in the sense that they are primary, they are above and beyond all else in the sense that they are the foundations of our personal identity, and they are the boundaries that contain and define our personhood, the very shape and structure of our psychic reality and stability.

Brigit's blankness, Patrick's shattered mind need help. They cannot help themselves. They are like someone who has lost the power of speech and cannot talk. What they have been presented with is too big for their mind to hold. Sometimes children, and this can persist into adulthood, are left with sensory fragments from the scene of the crime; a smell, an image, a sound, a taste, a bodily experience. Because they can't speak or think for themselves, we need to do so. What is a child to do when their hand is placed on a father's or a priest's penis and has sperm on it? What is sperm to Brigit or Patrick? Is the father/priest losing control of his bodily functions? Is he becoming incontinent? Is sperm another kind of urine? What sense do Brigit and Patrick make of the father's/priest's bodily movement during orgasm, his shaking, his increased heartbeat, the changes in his breathing? Is he ill? What's wrong with him?

The child's perception of the father's/priest's state – that he is ill and something is seriously wrong – may well be correct, because I would suggest that all men who abuse children suffer from a serious disturbance and in some cases are living on the edge of a breakdown. It is not their body that is malfunctioning: the more horrifying reality is that their mind is disintegrating even though their functioning may well appear as normal. In line with primary identifications, the child can be left with a sense of responsibility for the mental cohesion of the adult. This is an enormous anxiety for the child, particularly when it is actually the case that the adult 'needs' to abuse the child to defend himself against what he unconsciously perceives as a worse fate: personal mental disintegration. The child's sense of reality is challenged. The whole experience can lead the child to question their own grasp on reality.

While it is informative to place Brigit and Patrick side by side and learn about clerical child sexual abuse through parental child sexual abuse, we also need to consider clerical child sexual abuse separately.

Just as Brigit struggled with what was real, Patrick's struggle had enlarged into dimensions far beyond the reaches of a child's mind. He had to battle not just with the human but with the divine. A seven-year-old child cannot reach for thoughts that would make sense of a situation of such monumental dimensions. But he is in the presence of, and the privacy of his body has been intruded upon by, a sexually immature man whose ability to be intimately involved with another adult person is seriously deficient. It is very unlikely that he has had a sexual relationship with an adult woman, or man. A child like Patrick whose psychic life is threatened in an equivalent way to Bridget will do the same extraordinary things to survive: manage their mad world by dissociation, a denial or disavowal.

The sacraments in Catholic theology are the links to the Divine. The Reformation saw the hardening of attitudes in the narcissism of small differences. Small becomes large: in one, a direct contact with God is emphasised; in the other, the church (in the person of the priest) is the gateway through which you pass. The Catholic church strongly emphasised the latter with the priest as dispenser of sacraments. The priest (or bishop as priest) officiates at the significant stages of life. Birth (baptism), the move to adulthood (confirmation), marriage and death (extreme unction). He also administers to the essential activities of forgiveness (confession) and the Eucharist.

It's one thing to mess with someone's body.

It's another thing to mess with someone's mind.

It's yet another thing to mess with someone's soul.

Abusive priests have messed with children's souls. 'God,' Patrick was told, 'knows all things, past, present and to come, even your most secret thoughts and actions.' Diarmuid Martin made a start when he said betrayal of trust was compounded by the theft of self-esteem. The theft is of more than self-esteem.

Some people who grew up in the church and embraced it, but now no longer attend its rituals or concur with its beliefs, remain grateful for the good they found within it. In the next chapter, I will tell how the Irish writer John McGahern remembered and cherished sitting in the quiet of a church, the lambent sacramental light, the faint scent of incense evoked the eternal. He was always grateful to have had available a place of silence where refuge was found from the confusion, the pain, the loss and the violence of his childhood. When interviewed by Hermione Lee in 2004, he said,

> I'm very grateful in many ways to my upbringing in the church. It taught me a great deal about ceremony and mystery and sacrament and equality of all men and women under the sun. But I think it did an enormous amount of harm in sexual matters. It was a very puritanical church. It was a Romanesque church; a kind of fortress church. I think what should be a holy sacrament between people, sexuality, they turned into something dark and sinful. I said, when I was young, it was sort of witty but it was meant to be funny but it was kind of true as well – I said in Ireland it was a lesser sin to kill someone than it was to kiss them. And I think that's completely wrong myself.

Some were left with something. Some were left with nothing. Patrick was left with worse than nothing.

7

Intribo Ad Altare Dei

The resolution of these issues, an improvement in the situation, will not come about by shaming the church, although it is hard to see how that can be avoided. Its individual and collective crimes are immense. As the Murphy Report said,

> During the period under review there were four archbishops, McQuaid, Ryan, McNamara and Connell. Not one of them reported his knowledge of the sexual abuse of children by priests to the Gardai through the 1960s, 1970s or 1980s.

In 1987 McNamara took out insurance to protect the diocese financially, while not revealing the degree of clerical sex abuse recorded in diocesan files to the Gardai Siochana as required by law.

Understanding is essential. It's not everything. Without it, there's nothing. I am not very hopeful that new understanding, that insight will be sought and embraced. Insight can never be force-fed. A decree from on high will never bring it about. And it is hard work. As the Jesuit philosopher and theologian Bernard Lonergan said,

> ...even with talent, knowledge makes a slow if not a bloody entrance. To learn thoroughly is a vast undertaking that calls for relentless perseverance. To strike out on a new line and become more than a week-end celebrity calls for years in which one's living is more or less constantly absorbed in the effort to understand, in which one's understanding gradually works round and up a spiral of viewpoints with each complementing its predecessor and only the last embracing the whole field to be mastered.

I read these words, not just pertaining to someone developing original ideas, but the requirement of anyone who is to move beyond the place of obedience, a necessity for a church to reform itself.

There is a lot at stake here for the church. Take the policy that was adopted by many popes during the twentieth century. As mentioned earlier, in 1922 Pope Pius XI wrote a confidential memo about crimes of solicitation (*Crimen sollicitationis*). That memo required all investigations by the church of clerical abuse (homosexuality, bestiality, child abuse, soliciting sex in the confessional) to be carried out in strict confidentiality and dealt with inside the church. And the penalty for breaching confidentiality including reporting to the police, was automatic excommunication. Canon law in the twelfth century decreed that a priest who sexually abused a child was dismissed and handed over to the civil authorities. Pius XI's position was upheld in 1962 by Pope John XXIII and reissued with minor changes. In 1974, Pope Paul VI renamed *Secreta Continere* Pontifical Secret, that is, the Secret of the Holy Office. In 1983, Pope John Paul II imposed a five-year limitation period and in 1997 he restated the above and required bishops to send preliminary inquiries of cases of child sexual abuse to the Congregation for the Doctrine of the Faith. In all, six popes since 1922, three of whom have been made saints (the latest Paul VI in October 2018), have maintained and expanded the cover-up of child sexual abuse and the protection of the clergy.

The question I ask: does the Vatican now see that policy as a mistake? And if it does, what type of contrition would accompany its admission of mistakes?

I began this book recounting how in 2011 in the Irish parliament Enda Kenny delivered a scathing denunciation of the Catholic church which attempted to frustrate an inquiry into the rape and torture of Irish children by clergy. Enda Kenny said the Vatican had interfered in a sovereign democratic nation and the crimes of priests downplayed to protect the reputation of the church. Pope Benedict's reaction to the Cloyne report, Kenny said, was 'to parse and analyse it with the gimlet eye of a canon lawyer'.

Perhaps we can now understand Enda Kenny's fury more fully.

*

However, hope that the church has learned something about the issue was called into question when Bishop Lawrence Persico from the dioceses of Erie in Pennsylvania was interviewed on PBS *Newshour*, 17 August 2018. New information had come to light about the extent of the cover-up of priestly abuse by the church in Pennsylvania. Five other bishops in the state had declined interviews which suggested that Bishop Persico was one of the more enlightened clerics. He was clear that clerics who broke secular law should be accountable to that law, but when asked by Judy Woodruff to explain why the church had done nothing to protect children and instead protected the church, he said, 'there is no explanation'.

On 12 October 2018, Pope Francis accepted the resignation of Cardinal Donald Wuerl, who had presided over the church in Pennsylvania. In a letter to the cardinal, he said there was a difference between a cover-up of sexual abuse in the Catholic church and the official's 'mistakes'.

> You have sufficient elements to justify your actions and distinguish between what it means to cover up crimes or not to deal with problems, and to commit some mistakes. However, your nobility has led you not to choose this way of defence. Of this, I am proud and thank you.

Pennsylvania Senior Deputy Attorney General Daniel Dye, who was the lead investigator in the Pennsylvania probe, called out the pope's use of the word 'mistakes' and referred to 'Well documented, systemic, systematic, calculated, callous, insidious "mistakes"'.

Two months earlier, in August 2018, Pope Francis wrote a letter to Catholics worldwide. He criticised clericalism and spoke of the deep pain and powerlessness of children and survivors and recommended fasting and penance. Another leading Catholic commentator who appeared on PBS spoke of the need for contrition, and Kathline Spraws-Cummings of penitence and humility.

I do not accept that there is no explanation. In 2015, the documentary film *Spotlight*, on the work of the *Boston Globe*, exposed the scandal of clerical child sexual abuse in the Boston diocese and the cover-up by the Catholic church. Some said it was like an earthquake that rocked the Catholic church to its foundations. Maybe Pennsylvania is too far away to register any of the aftershocks!

In November 2018, a group of women theologians created a group called Voices of Change. The group was set up to publicise the sexual abuse of nuns by male clerics. One of the women who spoke at the first meeting was Doris Reisinger (Wagner). As a young nun in a mixed-gender catholic order, she was raped by the male superior. Her story was not believed. Her rapist still lives in a mixed-gender community. She was also groomed by a priest Hermann Geissler, who worked in the Congregation for the Faith at the Vatican. When this was exposed, he was reprimanded but not removed from his post, where he worked on child sexual abuse cases.

In her presentation, Doris Wagner referred to a report prepared twenty-five years ago by Irish nun Maura O'Donohue, who had assembled information of nuns abused by priests in twenty-two countries. This report was covered up. She also referred to a case where a priest got a young nun pregnant and then arranged for her to have an abortion. She died during the procedure. The priest officiated at her funeral mass.

In February 2019, the pope defrocked a convicted sex abuser, Cardinal McCarrick. A sign the Catholic church is beginning to take the issue in all its multiple manifestations seriously? I doubt it.

On 10 December 2019, Justice Peter McCellan, who had chaired the Royal Commission into clerical abuse in Australia, spoke publicly for the first time. An exhaustive seventeen-volume report was handed down in 2017. Speaking at the Australian Human Rights Commission and referring to the many Catholic church leaders who stated that sexual abuse of a child by a priest was a 'moral failure' rather then a criminal act, he said,

I cannot comprehend how any person, much less one with qualifications in theology…could consider the rape of a child to be a moral failure but not a crime. This statement by leaders of the Catholic church marks out the corruption within the church both within Australia, and it seems from reports, in many parts of the world.

And then, on 18 December 2019, Pope Francis announced his intention to abolish *Crimen sollicitationis,* the Pontifical Secret. Ninety-seven years after Pius XI wrote the secret memo, it is to be withdrawn. An acceptance that it was wrong? A sign of a more open church?

*

A final note on Brian Trevaskis. He trod on many toes, religious and secular. He was ahead of his time. Recently, an article in *The Irish Times* about ugly buildings described Galway cathedral as a 'squatting Frankenstein's monster' and 'a monument to the hubris of its soft-handed sponsors'. Trevaskis would be at home in modern Ireland, where in 2015 the Irish people voted in a referendum on the issue of marriage, whether 'marriage may be contracted in accordance with law by two persons without distinction as to their sex'. All major political parties and sixty-two per cent of voters supported the change. Ireland was the first country in the world to alter their marriage laws by popular vote. And in 2018 Ireland voted to change the anti-abortion laws.

Sometimes the rest of us are just playing catch-up.

*

The Sunday after Patrick was raped, he sat in the church pew listening to the sermon. The priest read from John's Gospel that 'God so loved the world that he gave up his only son so that those who believed in Him would have eternal life'. The priest said the incarnation was the cornerstone of all Christian belief. By adopting a human form, God dignified all people. The creator of the universe, all its far-flung galaxies and each nanoparticle of our material world and our bodies, became a human, thus dignifying all mankind. Our bodies, the body of every man, woman and child, were the temple of the Holy Spirit.

Where do we start to think about such a child as Patrick? I, in these chapters and throughout the book, offer many thoughts about the human mind and the care of that mind. Fundamental to it all is fostering that capacity to think. From the evidence that has been available to me, the church is still at a very elementary stage of understanding clerical child sexual abuse. In those interactions between priest and child, it is not just what is done, it is the feelings and fantasies that take place within the doing. The church's exploration of priestly sexual abuse seems to rarely go beyond what was done. I say that if we are trying to understand a child's subjective state and what happened to them, we must attend to how that state was constructed with another person. And we must attend to the way the divine has been drawn into all this. Bodies are damaged, minds are frozen in time, souls are desecrated.

*

Art has played an important role through the ages in constructing Christian mythology, not only on a grand scale but in shaping individual minds. You would not travel far on the roads of old Ireland without passing a shrine or signpost to a holy well. Shrines were predominantly of the Virgin Mary, often with Jesus and Joseph, the Holy Family.

Child sexual abuse in an actual family or in the larger family of the church shatters these images. Art and artists now have an important role to play in assisting thought about such fragmentation. When a person says, 'I can't believe Father So-and-so could do that to a child', they often can't imagine it.

Artists like Janet Mullarney have an important part to play. Her exhibition, The Perfect Family, featured family shrines. But instead of human forms in prayerful and expectant pose, her wooden life-size saintly figures in medieval dress are part animal, part human who care for and also devour their offspring.

The only art in which I have some talent is writing. And so I reach for poetic words to depict the way the saintly priestly figures in the Catholic church have devoured the young, the Patricks and the Brigits, of this world.

Introibo ad Altare Dei
I will go unto the altar of God. Psalm 42

Would to God
God's imposters
Raven-black
Blighted shadows
Spared the leaf
The stem the shoot
The fragrant
Flower of youth.

*

And what about Brigit? And what about the Brigits of this world who were fondled, photographed and raped by God's representative on earth?

Some, with good help, good fortune, will, to employ Ella Sharp's words, be witness to 'the incredible endurances and victories that some souls achieve over human fate'.

Others who are abandoned may live their life on the edge, unable to trust a sacramental sharing of their body and their mind with another human being.

Fringe Dweller

Staffs of life
Are to her abhorrent.
With unwavering gaze
And resolute lips
With hollow cheeks
And shrunken limbs
To numb her gnawing
Need she strides
With flailing arms
A moving crucifixion.

8

Out of the Valley of Darkness

As being ignorant of history makes us a slave to the immediate past, I, from time to time, take detours through Ireland's history. One is now called for.

The Catholic church in Ireland endured two great losses. One was inflicted upon it, the other it brought upon itself. Historians may rightly quibble at a swift glance over hundreds of years of history, but the following makes a valid point.

After the Viking raids, the next major influence on Ireland from outside was the Norman invasion in 1169. Having conquered England, their influence spread across the Irish Sea. (Actually, they were originally invited in by a disgruntled Irish chief whose power was waning.) The Norman influence contributed much, including the establishment of towns and urban establishments and all the social and cultural benefits that can bring. The Normans intermarried with the old Irish aristocracy and relative calm persisted until the sixteenth century. Up to that period, there was a beneficial interflow between aristocratic families in Ireland and England. Sons of Irish chiefs would spend time at the royal court in London.

Everything changed with the Reformation. The Irish had no need or wish to align with the new protesting order created in England by Henry VIII and others but were inevitably drawn into it, with disastrous results. The Williamite wars, the fight over the British crown between Protestant William of Orange and Catholic James were fought and concluded at the battle of the Boyne in 1691. (Anyone familiar with the troubles in Northern Ireland in the final decades of the twentieth century will know how enduring and deep-seated religious affiliations are.) The additional conflicts between the representatives of the British crown and various members of the Irish aristocracy led to the predictable defeat of the latter. The significant leaders on the Irish side left the country. Many went to Europe, mostly to France and Spain, and the migration, perhaps the first wave of Ireland's refugees, because known as the Flight of the Wild Geese or the Flight of the Earls.

Their departure left the country impoverished. All the working infrastructure of government, the executive and the administration, without which no state can operate, was gone. The Irish were then in position of being not only ruled by another country but instructed by that other country what to believe and think.

In establishing and maintaining its Empire, Britain devised ways to politically, economically and culturally control the 'natives' in whatever part of the world it conquered. Part of their success was that it tailored its approach to each new realm. Here in Australia, it was especially ingenious. It defined the land as *terra nullius*. An empty land belonging to no one! Australia is about the same size as Europe or the USA. At the time of writing, it has a population of twenty-five million. When the flag of Empire was first raised on Australian soil, it had an (approximate) population of one million. There were 400 nations and more than 600 languages. And the place had been inhabited for about 60,000 years.

With regard to the actual land of Ireland, the British effectively claimed it as its own. The Irish were dispossessed and the land given to English. These unjust 'plantations' caused long-lasting resentment. The most notorious was the plantation of Ulster at the end of the seventeenth century. It was a root cause of the troubles in Northern Ireland in the latter part of the twentieth century.

Throughout the seventeenth and eighteenth centuries Britain enacted a whole series of laws, called the Penal Laws, to economically and politically control the Irish. But they went a step further. They set out to control and eventually destroy Irish religious beliefs. Edmund Burke called the Penal Laws 'a machine of wise and elaborate contrivance, as well fitted for the oppression, impoverishment and degradation of a people, and the debasement in them of human nature itself, as ever proceeded from the perverted ingenuity of man'. Catholics in Ireland, as also in England at the time, were controlled and discriminated against. In Ireland, a Catholic not only had significant restrictions placed on religious practices, but was unable to engage in activities that economically advanced them. Education was restricted and the country, predominantly rural and peasant, was impoverished. Some Penal Laws, although obsolete, were still on the statute books in 1920.

In the midst of all this, the priest came to occupy a particular position in the Irish mind. A small number of the clergy was allowed and strictly controlled by the British government. They had to be registered and have a licence and were only permitted to operate in a restricted area. The policy makers hoped that over time there would be fewer and fewer priests and this would lead to the extinction of the Catholic religion in Ireland. But young men secretly went to the Continent, to places like Rome, Louvain, Salamanca. And they secretly returned as priests to a life of attending to the spiritual needs of the Irish, always with a price on their heads. A law of 1709 permitted the employment of priest hunters to seek out and arrest these priests. Nowadays, if you visit Ireland and get to know the local historians in the rural areas, they will tell you about places where in those dark days mass was celebrated. You may be shown the mass rock, a makeshift altar. Not far from my two-teacher school and the church are fields that even today are called Chapel Fields, where it is believed mass was secretly celebrated during the Penal Laws.

The Irish Privy Council in Dublin was responsible for monitoring priests in Ireland. It made recommendations to London on how issues should be handled. Following an internal subcommittee meeting in August 1719, the council wrote to London (27 August) relaying their deliberations. The letter read as follows:

Priests, Friars etc are no sooner transported but new ones come over from France, Spain or Portugal, so that their number continues as great as ever. The common Irish will never become Protestants or well affected to the Crown while they are supplied with priests, Friars etc. who are the fomenters and disturbers here. So that some more effectual remedy to prevent priests and friars coming into this kingdom is necessary, [our sub-committee proposed] the marking of every priest who shall be convicted of being an unregistered priest, friar etc and of remaining in this kingdom after the 1st of May 1720, with a large P to be made with a red hot iron on the cheek. We],The Privy Council generally disliked that punishment, and have altered it into that of castration which [we] are persuaded will be the most effectual remedy that can be found to clear this nation of the disturbers of the peace and quiet of the kingdom.

Neither of these proposals ever made it into law but I tell all this to make a point. The 'obedience' shown to the priest and the church was not some simple adherence to a set of beliefs. There was a long history where, in the absence of any political leadership, the priest carried the light of hope. And that the priest lived in constant danger of being found, transported or executed elevated him to a privileged place in the Irish psyche. Just as any country or individual person needs to learn about and comprehend their history if they are to understand the present, so we need to appreciate this history and include it in our understanding of the attitude of the people to its church and its priests.

Include all the above as you enter into the mind of 'Patrick' and 'Brigit', as you try to understand why such a child would find it hard to speak out for itself. Centuries of history and loyalty and resistance are in the drinking water!

We could at this point cast a sidewards glance at the Brexit debacle, playing itself out as I write. In my view, and I lived in England for more than twenty years, many voted in 2016 to leave Europe out of a sense of nostalgia for a past they believed to be important and which was in danger of being swallowed up by a European Union. Which past were they hankering for? What past are they knowledgeable about? Do they know what their 'England' did to Ireland?

Ireland's self-inflicted loss occurred in the nineteenth century. In the years following Catholic emancipation in 1829, plans were made to set up a Catholic university in Ireland. In 1852, John Newman, an English cleric, went to Dublin to carry out those plans. But the bishops in Ireland, including Cardinal Cullen, were distrustful of Newman and he left Dublin and returned to England.

My heavily annotated copy of Newman's *The Idea of a University* is always a joy to return to. I would if I could make it required reading for the chancellors of every university in the country. Newman taught and wrote that the study of one subject alone, to the exclusion of others, contracts the mind. Exposure to universal learning leads to an appreciation of the value of listening to others. When in a facilitating environment of learning, the student, he says,

> apprehends the great outlines of knowledge, the principles on which it rests, the scale of its parts, its lights and shades, its great points and its little, as he otherwise cannot apprehend them. Hence it is that his education is called 'liberal'. A habit of mind is formed which lasts through a life, of which the attributes are freedom, equitableness, calmness, moderation and wisdom... This is the main purpose of a university in its treatment of its students.

Newman believed that the priest's sole pursuit of things spiritual, and disregard of all other knowledge as inferior, pointed down a dangerous path. In England, he found himself in further trouble with church authorities, in particular Cardinal Manning. His approach to learning was perceived as steps on the broad path to the evils of modernism. As the historian Sean O'Faolain has noted, Newman 'was also denounced in Rome as the agent of Catholic Liberalism in England'.

When the Irish writer John McGahern (much more on him later) finished secondary school, he was not in a position to finance his studies at a university and was accepted to train as a primary school teacher at the Teacher Training College in Dublin. His fees and living expenses were paid for by the state and a job was guaranteed. At the college, there were no literary societies, no debating or drama societies. Only religious societies. You were expected to attend mass every day and religious devotions in the evening. If you missed them or showed any character defect, there was immediate expulsion. The quality of training was poor. 'We were,' he said, 'being trained as non-commissioned officers to the priests in running the different parishes throughout Ireland.'

Newman was well and truly gone and his spirit banished.

*

I have listened in to some discussions within the Catholic church during the early months of 2019 about the cause and cure of abusing clergy. Pope Francis said clericalism is a problem. We wait to find out how Pope Francis sees clericalism, how he defines it. He has called it an 'ugly perversion' but it is unclear what he means by that. Should there be a comprehensive inquiry, it will be of interest to know what the terms of reference are.

After days of torrential rain, a man opens his front door of his house, sees the street flooded, goes back in and declares a weather event. His neighbour opens his front door, sees the flooding and declares the climate has changed.

Where will Pope Francis start from? Clericalism is deeply ingrained in Catholic church history and culture. It replied to the protestations of Martin Luther by declaring that eternal truths are passed down through the Revelations of Sacred Scripture and Tradition. Note the capital 'T'. Its clerical class sees itself as the guardian of Tradition.

Clericalism is now an often-used word and provokes much head nodding. In one debate, a new voice emerged – not clericalism, but power; the priesthood has too much power. It was not long before heads nodded to power. It is instructive to keep an eye on the directions that debates can take. There is a survival instinct in every institution and when under threat, every institution reacts to protect, to perpetuate and to propagate itself. This happens knowingly and unknowingly, consciously and unconsciously. In debates where the way forward is unclear, it is a common feature to make a sideways move. No one has a solution, there is no leadership, and inspiration is lacking. As actual change is illusory, a feeling of change is created.

Clericalism, whether broadly or narrowly defined, is not the cause of the abuse of children by church figures. It is a cause. It has most probably caused the protectionism that has been rampant in the church. It has allowed church authorities, bishops, cardinals and popes to justify to themselves and each other their evasions, their obstructions of justice, their protection of perpetrators, their denials and the demonisation of those who dare to complain. It has been a significant factor in the perpetuation of abuse and in the embrace of ignorance. If you think that all the knowledge needed resides within the clerical class to which you belong, why would you bother to learn from other sources?

Clericalism at its worst was at play in Pius XI 1922 memorandum (*Crimen sollicitationis*). And it was continued and its position further entrenched by the six popes who maintained and ratified it during the twentieth century. As an implicit declaration that the sexual abuse of a child by a priest was not a criminal act, by placing such an act outside the laws of the state, it was an offer of impunity to offending clergy. To define such acts as due solely to spiritual failing was a measure of what limited thought was given to it. On the other hand, plenty of attention was given to hide such criminal acts and plenty of thought to protect the assets and the reputation of the Catholic church.

To be able to help Patrick and Brigit, the pope and all church authority figures have to become Patrick and Brigit. They need to spend time in their shoes. But more significantly, in their minds. Praying for someone is not enough, unless the prayer gets you started on the road to somewhere else. I'm on my way to somewhere.

I now ask why Pope Pius issued *Crimen sollicitationis* in 1922. My attempt to explain will take me back in the nineteenth century.

Homo sapiens would not deserve his name were he not curious and have within himself what Bernard Lonergan S.J. called 'an unrestricted desire to know'. Scientific advances and the refinements of scientific method in the nineteenth century fed this desire. Discoveries in all branches of science advanced at a pace. Many posed no threat to religious belief. Indeed, clerics were among those notable scientists. Some discoveries were more unsettling. For many Christians who believed the world was created in six days, or that woman was made out of the rib of man, as per Genesis, Darwin's evidence that it took many millions and billions of years caused disquiet.

My proposal is that the church retreated from the modern world and this had profound implications. *Crimen sollicitationis* was a retreat into itself and was a logical conclusion following a number of previous moves which I shall note.

In 1870, the First Vatican council declared the pope infallible. It was, at the time strictly defined, the canon lawyers would be quick to point out. But a detrimental side-effect was an elevation of the position of the pope and increased authoritarianism in the church and many Catholics saw the pope as having absolute authority on many issues. *Ex Cathedra*, the Latin phrase used in the decree, entered into common usage.

Newman was one of many denounced in Rome as the agent of modernism. The word modernism has many meanings and nowadays more commonly refers to artists and artistic trends. In the Catholic church of the latter part of the nineteenth century, in the beginning of the twentieth century, it had a specific connotation. 'Modernism' and 'modernist' were first used in 1879 by Pope Leo XIII, and modernism as a threat to faith was further dealt with by Pope Pius X in 1907 by the papal decree *Lamentabili* in July and the encyclical *Pascendi* in September. Beyond the simple concern that the faithful would put more trust in science and less in God, there were more complicated theological and philosophical strands. To make sense of the concerns of the church it is useful to show how the issues were played out in the lives of a few individuals.

*

George Tyrrell was born in Dublin in 1861 into an Anglo-Irish Protestant family. When he was twenty, he converted to Catholicism, entered the Jesuit order in England and became a priest. He taught philosophy at a Jesuit seminary but was removed from the post a few years later because his ideas were considered too radical. He became a staff writer on the Jesuit journal *The Month*.

He believed the Catholic church paid too much attention to religious obligation and external manifestation of religion and too little on the internal workings of God in the individual soul. He criticised the church's theological and spiritual doctrines that he believed were out of date and out of step with the minds and needs of modern man. He also critiqued church teaching on hell. He considered it cruel and unjust and that a certain 'temperate agnosticism' was required for intelligent faith.

Tyrrell was censored and removed from his writing job. He relocated to parish work in Yorkshire. There, the intellectual displayed other qualities and was a very caring and inspiring local priest and preacher.

He found a voice for continued expression of his thoughts by writing anonymously. But one of his pieces was published in an Italian paper and in 1906 he was expelled from the Jesuits. On 30 September and 1 October 1907, Tyrrell wrote a critique of *Pascendi* in *The Times*. He said the thinking of the church was based on a theory of science and on a psychology that seemed as strange as astrology to the modern mind. The first Vatican Council also issued a decree *Dei Filius* (24 April 1870) which argued, based on Romans 1:20 'that it was possible to know God using the light of reason from the created order'. Kant's assertion that God cannot be apprehended by reason had posed a huge challenge to pre-existing philosophies. Reason's powers had been over emphasised, he claimed, and this did no one any good. *Dei Filius* seemed like a push back against Kant. Anthony Carroll described the tensions modern philosophers like Tyrrell faced when they engaged with thinking like Kant's.

By entering into dialogue with Kantian philosophy, they [modernist Catholic thinkers] clearly ran the risk of allowing it to so structure their thought that in the end they would only mimic the secular world that they were attempting to evangelise. This is always the risk: that in entering into the cultural trends and thought patterns of an age, one becomes colonised by them.

Carroll also said that *Pascendi* 'constructed modernism as a straw man in order to defend a certain type of philosophy and theology that had been designated as official by the Catholic church'.

Was modernism as Carroll suggests a straw man erected by Rome? If yes, the next question is what went wrong? I would say, a failure to think, to allow new observations, new phenomena, new revelations to be considered. My view is that in its dealings with Tyrrell and Blondel and others, the church cornered itself as it did with Galileo. Wedded to the belief about the movement of the planets, it forced Galileo to withdraw his claims.

Through the nineteenth century, while the church was concerning itself with the 'evils' of modernism, another movement was gathering momentum, slow at first – like all such movements – but nonetheless a thing of substance. That movement concerned childhood and the rights of children. It involved, for example, new laws to prevent the exploitation of child labour in the Industrial Revolution. It involved the provision of compulsory education for all children. In time, the movement progressed to acknowledge a psychology of childhood. By that, I mean that the life of the mind of the child was a legitimate subject for exploration and understanding. At its heart was a basic belief: a child is a person. Repeat after me, or write it, a hundred times: a child is a person.

We can ask why the church turned away from such knowledge. I prefer to ask *how* the church turned away. Starting from that place leads us into the mind of the church to examine its theology. The doctrine of the incarnation is pivotal to Catholic teaching. God became man through the person of Jesus, who was fully divine and fully human.

More than a few heretics have been expelled for questioning or watering down that tenet. Or worse, expelled from life. Yet the goodness of humanity is expressed in humanism, the emphatic understanding of a fellow human being, in this instance, a child.

Here I lay the charge of mindlessness on the church. It was mindless of its own principles, its own beliefs, its own theology. Humanism in the church mind was subsumed in modernism, which we know was defined as evil, the work of the devil.

It is humane and laudable to fight for the rights of children not to work in factories, go down mines or up chimneys. But the internal life of the child's mind also requires care and attentiveness. Had the church embraced such knowledge and not closed its mind to an important human advancement, I think considerable abuse of the minds and hearts of children would have been prevented.

The history of Christianity is punctuated by periods of ignorance followed by a return to learning. During the Dark Ages, many clergy had become terribly ignorant. The end of the eleventh century saw a renewed interest in thinking and learning. It happened again in the sixteenth century and caused friction in the church that led to the Reformation. One impetus for renewal then was the formation of the Jesuits. Priests were schooled in secular subjects and were fifteen years in training.

In the nineteenth century, the world was changing rapidly. It is my view that the Catholic church, in its fear of modernism, turned away from new knowledge about childhood and thus became ignorant of all the knowledge psychology offered. Freud, the self-named 'Godless Jew', was one of the many thinkers who made valuable contributions to the understanding of childhood and the deeper appreciation that the child is a person. In fact, his views and those of many others, independent of him or inspired by him, are more 'Christian' than those held by many clergy referred to in earlier chapters, more in tune with the Beatitudes than many a sermon given in churches in Ireland throughout the 1950s and 60s.

If I had small hope the church might shift on this issue, that hope diminished when I read in the *Sydney Morning Herald*, 30 January 2019, that Pope Francis ruled out changes to the rule requiring priests to be celibate. 'Personally, I think celibacy is a gift to the church,' he is quoted as saying.

To focus on celibacy is like focusing on clericalism. Again, we move, or are moved, sideways. And here I am leading you to another starting point.

Celibacy is about abstaining from sexual relations with another person. The consequence of celibacy that most interests me here is abstaining from parenthood. Catholic priests are called 'Father'. The pope is called the 'Holy Father'. And yet, for more than a thousand years, no priest has been a father, a real 'father', a parent of a child. At least not officially!

Cardinal Ratzinger, later Pope Benedict XVI, who retired in 2013, entered the debate in April 2019. High on his list of causes for the sexual abuse of children by clerics is the sexual revolution of the 1960s. This, he reasoned, made paedophilia and pornography acceptable. This is astounding. To place the sexual assault of a child alongside viewing a naked sexual image of an adult lacks any sense of proportion. Are they equally bad in his eyes? Does he imply that an adult who looks at a sexual image of an adult can easily trip into sexually assaulting a child? The same sexual revolution permitted, he claims, an openly gay culture in seminaries and this contributed to the sexual abuse of children by priests. Once again, there is a false association. A person, priest or non-priest, who is homosexual is no more likely to be a paedophile than a person who is heterosexual.

Pope Francis is a man with a good heart. It reaches out to those who suffer. It listens. But sometimes it is followed by a retreat. As if the repressive calls from the Curia grow louder in his head and he listens to them.

There is hope when someone like Archbishop Mark Coleridge of Brisbane speaks.

For me over the years it's been a journey from seeing abuse as a sin, to seeing it as a crime and then finally seeing it as a culture – by which I mean abuse and its coverup were aggravated, and probably caused, by cultural elements in the Catholic church. It took me a long time to see that and to see therefore the need for cultural change if we are to go to the root of the crisis and not just treat the symptoms. We've come a long way, but the further we go, the further we see we have to go (*Sydney Morning Herald*, 20 February 2019).

Around the same time, Pope Francis described sex-offending clerics as 'tools of Satan'. That is not a step forward. It is a step backwards. It is a number of steps backwards. Was Noel Reynolds a 'tool of Satan'? It locates the origin of the problem in a myth. In doing so, the minds of priests who sexually abuse children are not explored and understood. The statement is a retreat to a position Mark Coleridge has said he has now abandoned, primarily seeing the sexual abuse of children by priests as a sin. Evil is a good word to describe an action, useful to emote outrage. But it explains nothing.

Apart from linking priests who abuse children with Satan, Pope Francis also suggested that those who criticise the Catholic church were doing the work of the devil. I will draw this chapter towards a close on a critical note. Perhaps more a note about criticism, about good damnation and bad damnation. We find it in the thought of John Keats and William Hazlitt.

The film *Bright Star*, which was directed by Jane Campion and in which Ben Whishaw played John Keats, much space is created for thought. Ben Whishaw read everything by John Keats and much that was written about him in preparation for the part. All this was background knowledge. It was Jane Campion, said he, who enabled him to bring it alive inside himself. He described her as

> a magical being. She has some way of looking right inside you and she can understand things about you that you don't understand yourself. She seems to know instinctively about the things that block you from doing your best work. She has a way of gently getting those things out of the way, so you open up.

In his life, John Keats had a magical companion. He didn't call him such but he helped Keats to do his best work. It was William Hazlitt. Hazlitt was to Keats what Campion was to Whishaw. When others savagely criticised Keats for his poetry and his politics, Keats looked to Hazlitt to help him to know himself, to deal with the blockages that got in the way of his doing his best work. Keats could appreciate the creativity, the originality and the genius of Hazlitt's criticism. In writing to the painter Benjamin Haydon in March 1818, Keats, sweeping through the negativism and the envy of a number of his contemporaries, wrote

> It is a great pity that people should by associating themselves with the finest things, spoil them... Hazlitt has damned the bigoted and blue-stockinged – how durst the man? He is your only good damner, and if ever I am damn'd – damn me if I shouldn't like him to damn me.

What did Keats mean by this? And what relevance does it have to the subject and the situation at hand in this chapter? To make some space, I am going to start from far out, somewhere that might feel beyond the horizon. Emily Dickinson often started out there, so I have a good teacher. Instead of having the words 'Abandon hope all ye who enter in' above the entrance to Hades, I would place 'Vanity, narcissism, egotism will lead you to blindness.' A church that is preoccupied with itself and its own protection is a church of vanity. Vanity rejects all the good damners.

*

It is often in the honest examination of a problem that the seeds of the solution begin to sprout. It is often too, in being aware of the damage done to minds, that we place ourselves in a good position to carry out repairs and make our way out of the valley of darkness.

Once upon a time, a rich property owner met a poor man with a beautiful wife. He slept with her and to conceal his actions used his power to place the poor man in a dangerous position where he lost his life. When he had married the widow and she was pregnant with their child, a confidant came to see him. He had a dilemma and wanted an opinion. A small shopkeeper within the rich man's vast empire, who had worked hard and honest all his life, had been tricked by a wily partner, lost everything and was destitute.

Priding himself on a sense of justice in business, the rich man was outraged, swore to right the wrong and demanded straight away to be given the offender's name. 'Who is he?' he asked.

'It is you, sir. You are the man.'

Here, told slant, is the Bible story of King David, Uriah and his wife Bathsheba and the prophet Nathan (2 Kings, chapters 11 and 12). David acknowledges his wrongdoings, repents and confesses and writes the great penitential Psalm 50.

Can we hope for a new penitential psalm written and read in all of Christendom?

*

This concludes the treatment of the issue of clerical sexual abuse. However, there are many strands from what has been addressed which will find their way into subsequent chapters. Chapter 11 is called Feathers on the Breath of God and attends to the important question of religion's place in our world today.

※ **Part Two**

9

Introduction

I have examined a significant issue, the scandal of clerical abuse of children in the Catholic church and explored how the anxieties and emotions that the issue generate, presents particular challenges. I have pointed to my concern about the damage inflicted on the minds of children when they are sexually assaulted and abused by representatives of their God. I set out to explore church figures and politicians and address the need to be well-versed in the art and craft of thought.

In part two, I move to what is involved in thinking. I will set out a case for poetry as a form of thought and will progress with that argument. I will also promote the argument that dreams and dreaming be given their rightful place within the art and craft of thinking.

And there is a final front I will open up. Throughout history, much knowledge and wisdom have found their way onto pages of books that were later classified as religious texts. Sacred scriptures introduce us to many great poets and storytellers. They offer understanding of the human condition and speak to what Wilfred Owen called 'the eternal reciprocity of tears', the universality of loss and suffering.

But a certain art and craft and care are called for if we are to engage with spirituality as a form of thought. I see it as such and will attempt to write about it as best I can in a chapter named To Infinity and Beyond. When I do so, it seems akin to traversing a snow-capped mountain range, where the trace of a diagonal might at any moment trigger an avalanche. However, I am not alone. You will hear John McGahern describe one of his books as 'not a novel but a religious poem' and that 'all art approaches prayer', while Emily Dickinson's work is suffused with spiritual references and frequently references God, eternity and heaven. I wonder sometimes, is she saying to us, read theology as you would read a poem?

It could be argued that the word 'mindless' is misplaced in describing abusing priests; that they use their minds to subscribe to views different from mine. However, at the heart of this book is an effort to get beyond so-called 'fake news' and explore 'fake thought'. We should remember the man, Donald Trump, who coined and popularised the phrase 'fake news', by the following words he said about himself.

> The day I realised it can be smart to be shallow was, for me, a deep experience… When you start studying yourself too deeply, you start seeing things that maybe you don't want to see…and if there's a rhyme and a reason… People can figure you out, and once they figure you out, you're in big trouble.

This book began with a memory of a four-year-old hand holding a pencil and tracing diagonals. We all need to start where we came from. Indeed, ignorance of childhood is a cardinal sin of a church that ignored, minimised and covered up sexual abuse in its ranks. One feature of the thinkers and writers I have so far mentioned, and those who will feature in this second part of the book, all keep in touch with their childhood. All are aware, for better or worse, of what has shaped their minds from their beginnings.

We all must learn to use our mind well. Despite formidable challenges, the future is essentially a hopeful one. We make a difference when we put our own mind in good working order. It is simple. Learn to think.

Except it's not simple. It is a profound and delicate enterprise. That is why I amass a host of figures to shore up my arguments and to school us in the art and craft and care of thought. And if our minds are in good shape, we are ready to tackle other issues that threaten and endanger the beauty of life on this most beautiful planet. Shakespeare said, 'So are you to my thoughts as food to life / Or as sweet seasoned showers are to the ground.' And today we need thoughts as food for our life. When good thoughts are defiled and debased by fake ideas, we must rebuild them. When rebuilt, we stand by and protect, because they are necessary and real. Good ideas and good thoughts are sweet seasoned showers that nurture our life.

10

On Going On a Journey with William Hazlitt

If Enda Kenny had been born four hundred years earlier, he might have come to a bad end. A few decades before Galileo was imprisoned and tortured by the Catholic church's Inquisition and forced to sign a document declaring the planet Earth was at the centre of the universe, another Italian, Giordano Bruno, came to a bad end. Bruno, a philosopher, mathematician and poet, said he had discovered the truth about the cosmos and the movement of the planets. When challenged, he refused to retract. Instead, he predicted that his discoveries would in time become common knowledge and declared, 'Time is the Father of truth; its Mother is our mind.'

Four hundred yeas ago in Italy, any distinction between church and state was non-existent. Knowledge about the material world was inextricably bound up with beliefs about heaven and earth, and the love preached by a man called Jesus from Nazareth replaced by a fundamentalist creed. Fail to assent to that creed and you risked being murdered by the church. In February 1600, Bruno was tortured. His face enclosed in an iron mask to prevent him from speaking, he was taken to Campo de'Fiori, Rome, and burned at the stake.

Fast forward to 2011 and Enda Kenny stands up in the Dail and reveals that the Holy See had tried to frustrate inquiry into the rape and torture of Irish children by clergy.

In the twenty-first century, the word fundamentalist has become bound up with Islam. Islamic fundamentalists have turned to violence to force unbelievers to accept their creed and are determined to exterminate all who don't. But fundamentalism is not the prerogative of a single religion, and if we accept that time is the father of truth, our own time will remind us that it is alive in the present in many forms in many religions. And if our mind is the mother of truth, we will recognise the presence of fundamentalism in many secular forms.

However, I do not wish to proceed by simply considering fundamentalism as a set of religious or secular beliefs. Instead, I here treat it as a state of mind and want to examine what type of thinking can take place within that mind.

In *The Pursuit of the Ideal*, Isaiah Berlin discussed how living by ideas can degenerate into a zealous desire for perfection that overrides compassion. Berlin cautions against a pursuit of perfection as a road to happiness. It is neither conceptually nor practically possible. He sees danger in a total submission to an external authority. Equally dangerous is the establishment within one's own mind of an authority that is impermeable to change and disallows examination by others.

> The notion of the perfect whole, the ultimate solution, in which all good things exist, seems to me not merely unattainable – that is a truism – but conceptually incoherent; I do not know what is meant by harmony of this kind. Some among the Great Goods cannot live together. That is a conceptual truth. We are doomed to choose, and every choice may entail an irreparable loss. Happy are those who live under a discipline which they accept without question, who freely obey the orders of leaders, spiritual or temporal, whose word is fully accepted as unbreakable law; or those who have, by their own methods, arrived at clear and unshakeable convictions about what to do and what to be that brook no possible doubt. I can only say that those who rest on such comfortable beds of dogma are victims of forms of self-induced myopia, blinkers that may make for contentment, but not for understanding of what it is to be human.

*

At the end of the eighteenth and the beginning of the nineteenth centuries, the England that was being shaped by three powerful events, the

French Revolution, the Napoleonic Wars and the Industrial Revolution, was not unlike Bruno's Italy of two hundred years earlier. What we identify as the age of Romanticism Coleridge called the 'age of anxiety'. In his maiden speech in the House of Lords in London in 1812, Lord Byron said, 'I have been in some of the most oppressed provinces of Turkey, but never under the most despotic of infidel governments did I behold such squalid wretchedness as I have seen since my return in the very heart of a Christian country.' When John Keats went walking in Scotland and Ireland in 1818 and observed the appalling poverty around him, he blamed the political system, pronouncing it 'a barbarous age'. Fearing or pretending to fear an insurrection, the government suspended habeas corpus, passed the Sedition Acts and William Pitt made the public discussion of public affairs a capital offence and his attorney-general said it was high treason for anyone to campaign for 'representative government'. While larger political freedoms were to be suppressed, so also were any moves by an increasingly industrialised and urbanised work force to organise and unionise itself. Anglicanism was the state religion and the universities excluded non-conformists. During the latter part of the eighteenth century, membership of religious groups like the Methodists, Baptists, Congregationalists and Unitarians increased dramatically.

A man who was born into those times and who made a significant contribution to the art and craft of thinking, whom you have already met, was William Hazlitt. Hazlitt's father, who was also called William, was born in Shrone Hill in County Tipperary, Ireland, in 1737. Excluded from Oxford and Cambridge because he did not belong to the established church, he went to Glasgow University and became a minister in the Unitarian church. His son William was born in Maidstone, Kent, in 1778. He spent parts of his childhood in Ireland and America before the family settled in Wem in Shropshire. In 1793, at the age of fifteen, he went to the Unitarian New College at Hackney, London, until its closure in 1796.

In 1798, he moved back to London to develop a career as a portrait painter. Commissioned to make copies of the great masters at the Louvre, in 1802, during a period of peace between France and England, he spent some months in Paris. On his return to England, he made a meagre living as an itinerant portrait painter and began to write. In 1805, his first publication appeared, a book on philosophy called *An Essay on the Principles of Human Action*. In 1812, he gave his first public lectures on English philosophy and got his first job as a parliamentary reporter with the *Morning Chronicle*. His writing and critical career began to expand with work for the *Champion*, the *Examiner* and the *Edinburgh Review*. By 1817, he was a major essayist, art and drama critic and political commentator. His writings are extensive and his collected works fill twenty-two volumes. He died in Soho, London, in 1830. He was fifty-two.

William Hazlitt shared Isaiah Berlin's concern about fundamentalism. Echoing Berlin (in words that have an eerie resonance for our times), he wrote,

> The most blind and bigoted belief is the most dogmatical; and those ages and nations which are the most ignorant, are most bent on writing the proofs of their faith in the blood of their enemies.

Hazlitt writes so well I hesitate to summarise or paraphrase him, so I decide to, when required, quote him at length. I was originally drawn not to his thinking as such, nor to his psychological perceptiveness, both of which are considerable, but to the beauty of his prose, his exquisite use of language. The first piece I read was from his reflections on Troilus and Cressida. Both Chaucer and Shakespeare wrote plays based on the same historical event. Hazlitt compared the two writers.

> Chaucer had a great variety of powers but he could only do one thing at once. He set himself to work on a particular subject. His ideas were kept separate, labelled, ticketed and parcelled out in a set form, in pews and compartments by themselves. They did not play into one another's hands, they do not react upon one another as the blower's breath moulds the yielding glass. There is something hard and dry in them. What is the most wonderful thing in Shake-

speare's faculties is their excessive sociability, and how they gossiped and compared notes together.

Hazlitt returned to the same subject in his Lectures on the English Poets, where he wrote,

> The striking peculiarity of Shakespeare's mind was its generic quality, its power of communication with all other minds – so that it contained a universe of thought and feeling within itself, and had no one peculiar bias, or exclusive excellence more than another. He was just like any other man, but that he was like all other men... The passion in Shakespeare is of the same nature as his delineation of character... The human soul is made the sport of fortune, the prey of adversity: it is stretched on the wheel of destiny, in restless ecstasy.

Hazlitt believed that it was necessary to examine your own mind, to scrutinise how you think. The heavy thought of care follows you wherever you go. Not content with outlining the consequences of fundamentalism, Hazlitt said the mind of the fundamentalist is not a mind apart from the rest of us. Listen to these lines plucked from various essays.

> Our unconscious impressions necessarily give colour to, and react upon our conscious ones; We are not hypocrites in our sleep...in dreams our passions and imagination wander at will... The griefs we suffer are for the most part of our own seeking and making... There must be a spice of mischief and wilfulness thrown in the cup of our existence to give it its sharp taste and sparkling colour... Each individual is a world to himself, governed by a thousand contradictions and wayward impulses... Every man, in reasoning on the faculties of human nature, describes the process of his own mind.

But on the issue of thinking, a stand-out line for me is reading the first sentence from his paper entitled *The Spirit of Philosophy*. Reading it was like opening the back of an old watch: a spring flickered like a spider's web; tiny wheels interlock and move to measure time. 'The spirit of philosophy consists in having the power to think and the patience to wait for the result'.

Hazlitt compared the mind at work to a dog searching for truffles. The dog is led by smell to the spot where the truffles are buried but has to dig down to find them.

> There is a certain air of truth which hovers over particular conclusions and directs our attention towards them, but it is only the acuteness and strength of the reasoning faculty that digs down to the roots of things.

The dog trusted his sense of smell; Hazlitt gave himself over to walking. Like many of his generation, he walked long distances out of necessity. But, as he told us in his essay *On Going a Journey*, to walk was something else.

> One of the pleasantest things in the world is going a journey; but I like to go by myself. I can enjoy society in a room; but out of doors, nature is company enough for me. I am then never less alone than when alone… I cannot see the wit of walking and talking at the same time. When I am in the country I wish to vegetate like the country… I like solitude, when I give myself up to it, for the sake of solitude… The soul of a journey is liberty, perfect liberty, to think, feel, do, just as one pleases. We go a journey chiefly to be free of all impediments and of all inconveniences; to leave ourselves behind much more to get rid of others. It is because I want a little breathing-space to muse on indifferent matters that I absent myself from the town for a while, without feeling at a loss the moment I am left by myself… Give me the clear blue sky over my head, and the green turf beneath my feet, a winding road before me, and a three hours' march to dinner – and then to thinking! It is hard if I cannot start some game on these lone heaths. I laugh, I run, I leap, I sing for joy… I plunge into my past being, and revel there… long-forgotten things…burst upon my eager sight, and I begin to feel, think, and be myself again. Instead of an awkward silence, broken by attempts at wit or dull common-places, mine is that undisturbed silence of the heart which alone is perfect eloquence.

I'm left wondering if our graffiti artist had read Hazlitt! The truth, as Emily Dickinson, who was born the year Hazlitt died, told us is best approached from an angle. 'Success in circuit lies.' Hazlitt's vegetating led him to common sense. Common sense is a mental sense of smell.

> Common sense or a certain tact may be said to be the foundation of the truest philosophy; for there is always a number of facts with a general impression from them treasured up in the memory, which it is the business of the understanding to examine, and not to cavil or contradict.

Hazlitt's first book, *Essay on the Principles of Human Action*, fell into oblivion shortly after publication. It was, for the most part, met with indifference and hostility. One reviewer described it as 'impious and illiterate'. Hazlitt always believed it was one of his most important works although he admitted it was 'tough and dry'. Others referred to it as 'that hard, dry, metaphysical choke-pear'. However, much of his later writings can be seen as developments of ideas he wrestled with in that text. The teeth and claws of the science are very much in evidence in this work. Writing on the need to keep the understanding free and the judgement unbiased, he said,

> a mistaken notion of simplicity has been the general fault of all system-makers, who are so taken up with some favourite hypothesis or principle, that they make it the sole hinge on which everything else turns and forget that there is any other power really at work in the universe; all other causes being either set aside as false and nugatory, or else resolved into that one. There is another principle which has a deep foundation in nature that has also served to strengthen the same feeling; namely, that things never act alone, that almost every effect that can be mentioned is a compound result of a series of causes modifying one another, and that therefore the true cause of any thing is seldom to be looked for on the surface, or in the first distinct agent that presents itself.

When we revisit a text written two centuries ago, it's important to note changes in language and how words are and were used. 'Science' first appeared in English in 1836. 'Psychology', as referring to the inner workings of a person's mind, was first used (by Coleridge) in 1834. When Hazlitt spoke about his interest in 'metaphysics', what he is often referring to is what we would call 'psychology'. When he refers to 'philosophy', he is often referring to an introspective philosophy. In *The Shyness of Scholars,* he wrote,

> Philosophy also teaches self-knowledge; and self-knowledge strikes equally at the root of any inordinate opinion of ourselves or wish to impress others with idle admiration.

Catherine Macdonald Maclean noted Hazlitt's interest in the 'under-conscious', with which 'his later essays are saturated and which constitutes one of their chief preservatives and one of the chief sources of their power to interest'. This is substantiated by Hazlitt, who wrote about 'the way in which I work out some of my conclusions underground, before throwing them up to the surface', and stated that he set out in his essays to write 'a sort of *Liber Veritatis,* a set of studies from human life'. Because man is an intellectual animal, he is an everlasting contradiction to himself. 'His senses centre in himself, his ideas reach to the ends of the universe; so that he is torn to pieces between the two, without a possibility of it being otherwise.'

If we need further clarification as to what falls under the rubric of 'metaphysics' and 'philosophy', as Hazlitt conceived of them, we can turn to his own words:

> Physical experience is indeed the foundation and the test of that part of philosophy which relates to physical objects...but to say that physical experiment is either the test or source or guide of that other part of philosophy which relates to our internal perceptions, that we are to look to external nature for the form, the substance, the colour, the very life and being of whatever exists in our minds, or that we can only infer the laws which regulate the phenomena of the mind from those which regulate the phenomena of matter, is to confound two things entirely distinct. Our knowledge of mental phenomena from consciousness, reflection, or observation of

their corresponding signs in others is the true basis of metaphysical inquiry, as the knowledge of facts, commonly so called, is the only solid basis of natural philosophy.

Common sense, Hazlitt tells us, 'may be said to be the foundation of the truest philosophy' because it picks up the scent of what is true. He also refers to 'a certain tact', 'prejudices', 'fancy', 'natural feeling and inclination', 'lax and loose beliefs'. All of the above are not merely irritants that we have to tolerate in ourselves and others. They are not to be discarded as extraneous factors. They perform vital functions, not least because they can act like the dog's nose and take us to what we need to think about.

If we endeavour to shut out and suppress all natural feeling and inclination to one side of a question rather than another, this will be more likely to warp and precipitate our judgment, and make us impose false and premature arguments upon ourselves as the true, in order to get rid of so uneasy and artificial a state.

Words, as I have said, through the centuries, can acquire new and divest old meanings. Some, like 'meek', lose a sharpness, while others, like 'prejudice', acquire an edge. 'Meek' now has a stress on passiveness and submissiveness, but used to describe kindness, being merciful and courteous. 'Prejudice' in Hazlitt's day meant a preconceived opinion not one based on actual experience.

John Keats echoes Hazlitt's principles when in a letter to a friend he described a man named Dilke as incapable of 'being in uncertainties, mysteries, doubts, without any irritable reaching after fact and reason'. He also said that Coleridge 'would let go by a fine isolated verisimilitude caught from the Penetralium of mystery, from being incapable of remaining content with half knowledge'.

Hazlitt not only enjoyed great company, he enjoyed the privacy of his mind and the solitude in nature. Like Heaney's poems, his essays have an earthiness within which profound thought grows.

Our understanding…is not a thoroughfare for common places,

smooth as the palm of one's hand, but full of knotty points and jutting excrescences, rough, uneven, overgrown with brambles; and I like this aspect of the mind (as someone said of the country), where nature keeps a good deal of the soil in her own hands.

In *The Spirit of Philosophy*, concerned he is tiring the reader with his metaphysical choke-pear talk, Hazlitt elides into poetry. He turns to Wordsworth's *Lyrical Ballads* and says,

I shall relieve the dryness of this description by quoting the lines,

> The eye – it cannot choose but see;
> We cannot bid the ear be still;
> Our bodies feel where'er they be,
> Against or with our will.
>
> Nor less I dream that there are powers,
> Which of themselves our minds impress:
> That we can feed this mind of ours,
> In a wise passiveness.

With a mind refreshed, we can distil the essence of Hazlitt's thought about the way humans are connected to each other. He believed in disinterestedness. We go out of ourselves into another human being, we go beyond selfish concerns and thereby connect with others. The needs and interests of others are the same as ours. Through sympathy and empathy, we transcend ourselves and are enriched. When reading the thoughts of others, our mind melts into their mind. We lose ourselves in the same way as we lose ourselves in nature. We let the thoughts and emotions of another react upon us as the blower's breath moulds the yielding glass. Through this form of creative imagining, our minds are enriched.

*

Taking care with thought is the oxygen of a decent world. Without thinking, beliefs become ossified; they shrivel into creeds, systems and dogmas. Dictators, religious and secular, and their foot soldiers, are always on standby. *Fidei Defensor.*

This book began with intent to address this situation. And the solutions that are offered are not premised on acquiring a dictator-like power to engage in combat – the irresistible force meeting the immovable object. My starting point was inside my own mind and I'm suggesting your starting point be inside your mind. You and I are more efficient, formidable and enduring agents for promoting love and protection of our world when we respond rather than react.

Technology and globalisation mean we live in a time of change. Some call it unprecedented. Here, a certain vanity or affectation can creep in. We only need to scratch the surface of history to learn that we are not alone. Others who have gone before have faced issues very familiar to us now. And some of them had thoughts and solutions that, if known and listened to, pay a good dividend. Some people transcend time. And they speak afresh. Someone told me they read *Hamlet* every ten years and wonder how it is that Shakespeare has managed to rewrite the play every time. Hazlitt's words transcend time. In my view, he combines those two qualities that I earlier described as residing in Chaucer and Shakespeare: to be rigorously systematic and imaginatively explorative. And if I can beg patience, I may carry on for a while longer unpacking what William Hazlitt has to offer us.

One of the benefits of reading good writers is that, beyond their gifts as storytellers and wordsmiths, some possess the gift of seeing deeply into the minds of people. In other words, they are perceptive psychologists. Not content with the externals of a person's behaviour, they probe deeply into the mind of Man. And in their study of Man, they examine their own mind. In fact, their own mind is a regular port of call. I have consistently argued to the necessity of thinking if we are to know and love the world and ourselves. Hazlitt's psychology is full of dynamic perspectives. To date, I have referred to four significant people from the world of psychoanalysis: Sigmund Freud, Ronald Fairbairn, Hans Loewald and Ella Sharpe. But Hazlitt anticipated much of what these thinkers articulated for us in the twentieth century. In 1920, L.C. Martin from the Sorbonne published a paper in *The International Journal of Psychoanalysis* called 'A Note on Hazlitt'. Martin listed many aspects of Freud's thought that were present in Hazlitt's writings, including repression, denial, projection, introjection, the importance of childhood and infantile life and dreaming, and he added,

> A more than usually sustained habit of enquiry and gifts of insight and analysis much beyond the average gave to Hazlitt's Freudian suggestions something like the character of a consistent and dynamic though loosely woven theory of the unconscious.

He continued,

> These sporadic anticipations furnish a striking instance of the manner in which a whole new system may remain latent in the mind of an individual and without influence on the progress of human thought and society, for lack of the will or the opportunity to carry an original idea to its final and logical conclusions. Yet though Hazlitt did not attain, it is something that he experienced and bore witness to an unusually clear vision.

I have already given some instances of that vision. I will now extend that. In 1815, in an essay, 'Mind and Motive', Hazlitt wrote,

> We waste our regrets on what cannot be recalled, or fix our desires on what we know cannot be attained. Every hour is the slave to the last; and we are seldom masters either of our thoughts or of our actions... Even in the common transactions and daily intercourse of life, we are governed by whim, caprice, prejudice, or accident. The falling of a tea-cup puts us out of temper for the day; and a quarrel that commenced about the pattern of a gown may end only with our lives... We are little better than humoured children to the last, and play a mischievous game at cross purposes with our own happiness and that of others.

One of Hazlitt's earliest biographers, Alexander Ireland, pointed to the centrality of introspection or self-analysis in his understanding of himself. Describing the coaching inn at Winterslow Hutt on the border of the Salisbury Plains where Hazlitt wrote many of his essays, Ireland wrote,

> It was his favourite haunt when he wished to secure that entire solitude and seclusion from the world which he found so favourable to thought and quiet literary work. It was here that he drew upon his recollections of books and pictures, recalling what he had observed of men and things, probing his own character unshrinkingly, and extracting an infinite amount of self-knowledge from his own infirmities.

When he was forty-two, Hazlitt's marriage was falling apart. He moved out and lived in a boarding house, where he fell madly in love with Sarah Walker, a girl half his age. This was one of the most painful times of his life. He would later write a famous, some would say infamous book, *Liber Amoris*, about those years. Divorce was then illegal in England. He went to Edinburgh, where it was as legal. He came back by steamboat. He wrote this letter to a friend.

> A raging fire is in my heart, that never quits me. The steam-boat (which I foolishly ventured on board) seems like a prison-house, a sort of spectre-ship, moving on through an infernal lake, without wind or tide, by some necromatic power – the splashing of the waves, the noise of the engine gives me no rest, night and day – no tree, no natural object varies the scene – but the abyss is before me, and all my peace lies weltering in it! I feel the eternity of punishment in this life; for I see no end of my woes… I am tossed about (backwards and forwards) by my passion, so as to become ridiculous. I can now understand how it is that mad people never remain in the same place – they are moving on forever, *from themselves*.

*

Hazlitt would challenge his own side of politics when they only spoke to like-minded people and only read their own writings. His appreciation of how groups and sects and parties operate and his challenge to the faithful to always account for themselves and be aware of their proximity to hypocrisy meant that he could be a lone voice and not a very popular one at that. He exposed the zealots in whatever form they appeared, whatever garments they donned in the essay 'On Party Spirit' when he wrote,

> We may be intolerant even in advocating the cause of toleration, and so bent on making proselytes to freethinking as to allow no one to think freely but ourselves. The most boundless liberality in appearance may amount in reality to the most monstrous ostracism of opinion – not condemning this or that tenet, or standing up for this or that sect or party, but in a supercilious superiority to all sects and parties alike. And prescribing, in one sweeping clause, all arts, sciences, opinions, and pursuits but one's own.

Hazlitt wrote stridently against slavery. He campaigned for Catholic emancipation. He believed that the treating of a minority in an uncivilised manner was a sign of a primitive or a collapsed civilisation. Writing about the Jewish madam who controlled the young prostitutes around the theatres in London, Hazlitt detested her abuse of them, but as always has an eye to the larger picture:

> Shut out any class of people from the path to fair fame, and you reduce them to grovel in the pursuit of riches and the means to live… You tear up people by the roots and trample on them like noxious weeds, and then make an outcry that they do not take root in the soil like wholesome plants, you drive them like a pest from city to city, from kingdom to kingdom, and then you call them vagabonds and aliens.

Hazlitt strongly criticised the poet laureate Robert Southey in 1818. Southey was actively supporting the right-wing Tory government in their suspension of habeas corpus and the passing of the Sedition Act. Southey referred to Hazlitt and his fellow radical Leigh Hunt as men who 'live by calumny and sedition; they are libellers and liars by trade', and said that they should be arrested and transported. How would we react today if we read Southey's words (written in 1814) calling for the French to be castigated as 'the Jews of Europe, a people politically excommunicated and never to be forgiven, and above all never to be trusted'.

In 1803, when England again declared war on France, Hazlitt condemned the general warmongering which was in fashion and in particular the activity of Wordsworth, who in his sonnets was calling the nation to war and to its supposed glories. To Hazlitt, this was an example of a long narrowing of the mind. A nation must defend itself and Hazlitt did not exempt himself from playing a role in such an emergency. What he most criticised was extolling of the glory of war and taking delight in the destruction of one's fellow man. When this point is reached, everyone becomes a loser. Men have lost the awareness of their common humanity. This was an issue central to Hazlitt's politics. He did not believe that wrongs would right themselves. 'Society,' he wrote, 'when out of order, which it is whenever the interests of the many are regularly and outrageously sacrificed to those of the few, must be repaired, and either a reform or a revolution cleans its corruptions and renew its elasticity.'

As suggested, under the influence of his father, Hazlitt's political sensitivities were honed at an early age. At the age of fifteen, he wrote to his mother about a visit while on holidays in Liverpool to a certain gentleman's house.

> He is a very rich man, but – the man who is a well-wisher to slavery, is always a slave himself. The King, who wishes to enslave all mankind, is a slave to ambition. The man who wishes to enslave all mankind for his king is himself a slave to his king.

*

Consider the people of the world. Consider the forms of government they live under. Consider Russia, ruled by a despot under a false definition of democracy. Opposition is stifled, leaders arrested and journalists jailed or murdered. In China, those who belong to the Communist

Party, a secret organisation – 7% of the population – control the other 93%; a country where Liu Xiaobo was imprisoned for writing poems, who was denied proper medical help and hastily, when he died in 2017, buried at sea. Countries like Dubai and Saudi Arabia, behind the face of modernity, run police states (not unlike the post-Waterloo England) where peaceful dissent is not tolerated and most women are barely slaves. The list is long. From 200 years away, Hazlitt's voice is fresh and strong.

> I am no politician, and still less can I be said to be a party-man: but I have a hatred for tyranny, and a contempt for its tools; and this feeling I have expressed as often and as strongly as I could. I cannot sit quietly down under the claims of barefaced power, and I have tried to expose the little arts of sophistry by which they are defended. I have no mind to have my person made a property of, nor my understanding made a dupe of. I deny that liberty and slavery are convertible terms, that right and wrong, truth and falsehood, plenty and famine, the comforts or wretchedness of a people are matters of perfect indifference. That is all I know of the matter; but on these points I am likely to remain incorrigible, in spite of any arguments that I have seen used to the contrary. It needs no sagacity to discover that two and two make four; but to persist in maintaining this obvious position, if all the fashion, authority, hypocrisy, and venality of mankind were arrayed against it, would require a considerable effort of personal courage, and would soon leave a man in a very formidable minority… This is the only politics I know; the only patriotism I feel. The question with me is, whether I and all mankind are born slaves or free. That is the one thing necessary to know and to make good: the rest is *flocci, nauci, nihili, pili*. Secure this point, and all is safe: lose this, and all is lost.

*

I concluded chapter 8, Out of the Valley of Darkness, with a promise to take up the issue of criticism and respond to Pope Francis likening the work of the church critic with that of the devil. I postponed offering a reply because I had nothing to say. Some questions are posed and replies expected, but the questioner's frame of reference is so narrow there is little to be gained by even attempting an answer. The only way forward and out of these tight corners, as far as I can see, is to present broader terms of reference in the hope that within them discussion can recommence. Some might call it the establishment of a new paradigm. Providing substantial indications of how Hazlitt thought, and following with a gesture not unlike that envisaged by Pope John XXIII to bring fresh air into a fortress church, I have laid out enough to allow me to make an honest reply.

To have a right to criticism, to be a good damner, to refuse to walk down the road of obedience is the cornerstone of thought. Without it, everything crumbles. We need the Hazlitt whom Coleridge described as 'a thinking, observant, original man…[who] sends well-headed and well-feathered thoughts straight forwards to the mark with a twang of the Bow-string…says more than any man I ever knew…that is his own in a way of his own'.

Observant, original minds are called for. Hazlitt gave a good description of such a mind when he described his friend Joseph Fawcett, a Unitarian minister.

> I have heard [Fawcett] explain 'That is the most delicious feeling of all, to like what is excellent, no matter whose it is'. In this respect he practised what he preached… There was no flaw or mist in the clear mirror of his mind. He was as open to impressions as he was strenuous in maintaining them. He did not care a rush whether a writer was old or new, in prose or in verse – 'what he wanted' he said 'was something to make him think'… He gave a cordial welcome to all sorts, provided they were the best in their kind. He was not fond of counterfeits or duplicates. His own style was laboured and artificial to a fault, while his character was frank and ingenuous in the extreme… Men who have fewer native resources, and are obliged to apply oftener to the general stock, acquire by habit a greater aptitude in appreciating what they owe to others. Their taste is not made a sacrifice to their egotism and vanity, and they enrich the soil of their minds with continual accessions of borrowed strength and beauty.

Sometimes, those who espouse beliefs different from yours are not enemies. In fact, they may be your best allies. If their thought about us rises to the standard set by Joseph Fawcett, how can we lose? He wouldn't care a rush who you were, as long as you offered something that deserved thought. Being in the presence of such a person seems an honour. Personally, my only worry would to be ignored, as it would suggest I had nothing of interest to contribute.

One historical instance of clericalism at work protecting its power and privilege and the superiority of its class was the translation of the Bible from Latin into the language of the people. With the invention of the Gutenberg printing press in 1439, it was no longer necessary to hand-copy books. They could be mass-produced. English translations of the Bible, or parts of it, caused major upsets in the Christian churches. Their position threatened, the clergy punished the translators and owners with imprisonment, torture and death. William Tyndale, who translated the Bible into English, was imprisoned, executed by strangulation and his body burned at the stake by the Catholic church in Antwerp in 1536.

To listen to or to read the Bible stories and poems in your own language removed the clerical class from the position of translator and sole commentator. Hazlitt said the translation enabled the great work of liberating men's minds.

> It threw open, by a secret spring, the rich treasures of religion and morality…it revealed the visions of the prophets, and conveyed the lessons of inspired teachers.

Hazlitt attended the Unitarian College in Hackney. The universities were closed to dissenters and these who did not profess the Anglican/state faith. Lack of funds led to its closure, as did its failure to produce an adequate number of ministers of religion. The liberal education provided was held responsible by some for many of the young men losing their faith and the place was dubbed by Henry Crabb Robinson as 'the slaughterhouse of Christianity' – Hazlitt is reported by him to have left the place 'an avowed infidel'.

Hazlitt suggested Jesus should be of interest whether one was interested in theistic religion, natural religion, philosophy, humanity or true genius. He saw in Jesus disinterestedness writ large, someone who reached out to others in sympathetic identification. 'He redeemed man from the worship of that idol, self.' This concurs with Hazlitt's understanding of vanity and affectation and its central position in determining the quality of human life. In Hazlitt's view, redemption was dependent upon a resolution of one's vanity and narcissism. Human redemption is the capacity to see beyond oneself, to escape from the idolatry of our own being. Those who, when they look around themselves, forever see a reflection of themselves are blind to what is behind them. Hazlitt is not shy to use such phrases as the spark of divinity in mankind because he is thus referring to a world larger than one's self. The peace that he saw embodied in Jesus was a peace and happiness which followed from the ability to think about other people. A loving act arises from an accurate perception of the needs of someone else and is not measured by whether in the performance of a good deed it makes one feel good.

Hazlitt saw the Christian gospel as proclaiming the equality and dignity of all people. If Hazlitt is 'an infidel', and you were called to declare your allegiance, with whom would you align yourself? Are these the words of an infidel?

> There is something in the character of Christ too (leaving religious faith quite out of the question) of more sweetness and majesty, and more likely to work a change in the mind of man, by the contemplation of its idea alone, than any to be found in history, whether actual or feigned. This character is that of a sublime humanity, such as was never seen on earth before nor since. This shone manifestly both in his words and actions... He was the first true teacher of morality; for he alone conceived the idea of a pure humanity. He redeemed man from the worship of that idol, self, and instructed him by precept and example to love his neighbour as himself, to forgive our enemies, to do good to those that curse us and despitefully use us. He taught the love of good for the sake of good, without

regard to personal or sinister views, and made the affections of the heart the sole seat of morality, instead of the pride of the understanding or the sternness of the will... The gospel was first preached to the poor, for it consulted their wants and interests, not its own pride and arrogance. It first promulgated the equality of mankind in the community of duties and benefits. It denounced the iniquities of the chief priests and pharisees, and declared itself at variance with principalities and powers, for it sympathises not with the oppressor, but the oppressed. It first abolished slavery, for it did not consider the power of the will to inflict injury, as clothing it with a right to do so. Its law is in good, not power. It at the same time tended to wean the mind from the grossness of sense, and a particle of its divine flame was lent to brighten and purify the lamp of love!

I think the notion of vanity and affectation can be productively explored alongside the notion of clericalism. Is clericalism a form of vanity? As counterpoint to the figure of Jesus, we have in Hazlitt's writings a depiction of the opposite. In his essay 'On Living to Oneself', he borrowed a character from one of the novels of Samuel Richardson, Sir Charles Grandison, to describe an excessively egotistical person. He wrote,

> Some satirical critic has represented Grandison in Elysium bowing over the faded hand of Lady Grandison – he ought to have been represented bowing over his own hand, for he never admired anyone but himself, and was the God of his own idolatry.

*

John Keats welcomed Hazlitt's damning because he knew Hazlitt loved. And he knew the sentiments behind Hazlitt's criticism, which were later expressed by Rilke.

> Works of art are of an infinite loneliness and with nothing to be so little grasped as with criticism. Only love can grasp and hold and fairly judge them.

In 1543, Copernicus wrote a letter to Pope Paul III.

'I can easily conceive, most Holy Father,' he said, 'that as soon as some people learn that in this book which I have written concerning the revolutions of the heavenly bodies, I ascribe certain motions to the Earth, they will cry out at once that I and my theory should be rejected.

Loving a church to the point of idolatry creates a fatal flaw line that can bring down the whole edifice. A church that looks solely inside itself for solutions to its problems will remain in a valley of darkness. As E.M. Forster gave two cheers to democracy, the faithful of any church or religious institution should give two cheers only to their good-enough institutions. Imagine how things could have been different in Ireland if that had been so.

Can I give Shakespeare the closing words?

> Let not my love be called idolatry,
> Nor my beloved as an idol show,
> Since all alike my songs and praises be
> To one, of one, still such, and ever so.
> Kind is my love to-day, to-morrow kind,
> Still constant in a wondrous excellence;
> Therefore my verse to constancy confin'd,
> One thing expressing, leaves out difference.
> Fair, kind, and true, is all my argument,
> Fair, kind, and true, varying to other words;
> And in this change is my invention spent,
> Three themes in one, which wondrous scope affords.
> Fair, kind, and true, have often liv'd alone,
> Which three, till now, never kept seat in one.
>
> Sonnet 105

11

The Best Lived Quietly – Meeting John McGahern

Enda Kenny's speech in the Dail in 2011, when looked at in the flow of Irish history, was an act of great courage. It was also an act of great insight. He, a practising Catholic, knew that a fusion of church and state, quite apart from the crimes and corruption it permitted, was an act of blindness. Those who allowed it to develop and failed to execute a separation damaged both. A church should serve the spiritual; a state works to promote the secular. His speech was a defining moment in the story of Ireland.

I think moments such as this always require an individual to take a leap of faith. A creative spark strikes and ignites. But the spark doesn't arrive from nowhere. The act of creativity, if it ignites to effect substantial change, is built on foundations that often are years of thought in the making. In addition, others will have assisted in laying those foundations.

In 1966. when the furore around Brian Trevaskis was playing itself out on television and in the newspapers, another significant issue unfolded quietly in Dublin and involved a thirty-two-year-old teacher called John McGahern. McGahern was born in 1934. He worked in a primary school in Dublin. In his spare time and during school holidays, he taught himself to write. Freud had conveyed to Arthur Schnitzler that the writer's task is to be an explorer of the depths, and sometimes involves taking to pieces the social conventions of society. Most societies do not take kindly to in-depth examination of their conventions, and the new Irish society set in place by the establishment of the Irish Free state in 1922 was particularly wary of writers. In 1926, the Committee on Evil Literature was established. De Valera had stated that the arts in Ireland were to be encouraged when they observed the 'holiest traditions', but should be censored when they failed to live up to that ideal. Aldous Huxley's *Brave New World* was banned in 1932 and J.D. Salinger's *Catcher in the Rye* in 1951. In 1962, Edna O'Brien's *The Lonely Girl* was banned. James Joyce's *Ulysses* wasn't banned but a technical loophole allowed the government to prevent its importation into the country.

In 1966, McGahern published *The Barracks*. This was his second novel. His first, *The Dark*, completed in 1963, impressed Faber & Faber, but McGahern was reluctant to publish it at the time, believing he could do better. In *The Barracks*, Elizabeth the central character is a young Irish woman who leaves Ireland to work as a nurse in London. She had grown up in a rural community where the church dominated life, where to develop a mind of your own seemed impossible. Social conventions kept women in their place. De Valera's St Patrick's Day speech highlighted men, the single reference to women his phrase, 'happy maidens'. The written version sent ahead of transmission to RTE radio had referred to 'comely maidens'.

As one of the 600,000 Irish men and women then working in England, 'Elizabeth' did not consider herself a happy maiden. She wanted a measure of economic freedom. But she sought another freedom. She borrowed books from the public library beside Aldgate East Station. She fell in love with Halliday.

> The impossible became turned by fierce desire into the possible, the whole world beginning again as it always has to do when a single human being discovers his or her uniqueness, everything becoming strange and vital and wondrous in this the only moment of real innocence, when after having slept for ever in the habits of other lives, suddenly, one morning, the first morning of the world, she had woken up to herself.

Elizabeth is a creation of John McGahern's mind. But the writing of her, the writing of the whole novel, was also a personal statement. In the years conceiving and planning the novel, he not only learned the art and craft of writing, he put himself in the company of other great writers: Proust, Beckett, Chekhov, Yeats, Tolstoy and many others. But he had been born into and came out of the same world as Elizabeth. The church dominated his world. He was acutely aware of the position of those who spend a significant part of their life observant, who have cut themselves adrift from traditional beliefs and pieties and struggle to feel or articulate a clear purpose in life and found themselves disorientated when they moved from under those constrictions.

McGahern won awards and a name with *The Barracks*. Following its success, Faber & Faber published *The Dark*. The novel was deemed pornographic and banned. The censorship board saw references to masturbation and child sexual abuse, although somehow, they failed to use the word sex while banning it. That he was working as a teacher in a Catholic school in Dublin was an embarrassment to the authorities. They were doubly indignant when it was discovered that, contrary to Catholic teaching, he had married a divorced woman in Finland. Advised by his educational superiors to resign from his job, he refused and sought assistance from the teachers' union but he was told, 'If it was just the auld book, we might have been able to do something, but marrying this foreign woman you have turned yourself into an impossible case entirely.' Archbishop McQuaid then sacked McGahern from his job. McQuaid had taken an active part in ensuring the new novel was banned and complained personally to then Justice Minister Charles Haughey, saying *The Dark* 'was particularly bad'.

McQuaid had earlier presented himself to the management of RTE and demanded control of the religious programming. He was politely told it was not his business and the station maintained its independence. Some people were beginning to speak out but McGahern left Ireland to live abroad. Some of his fellow writers considered objecting to the ban. Samuel Beckett, who then lived in Paris, asked McGahern if he wanted open support. McGahern declined the offer. He believed such an action would convey legitimacy on the (1960s version of the) Committee on Evil Literature, which it did not deserve.

When McGahern's *Memoir* was published in 2005, it was clear that he had transformed the raw materials of his own life and moulded them into his (six) novels and his short stories. His father's harshness, which sometimes developed into violence, and his mother's death from cancer when he was ten, presented serious challenges. These difficulties were partly mitigated by access to a private library. Books provided solace and space for him to live and grow within. Some of the seeds of gratitude and excitement about books that he dramatised in the conversations between Elizabeth and Halliday were sown in that library.

After living abroad for ten years, McGahern returned to Ireland and bought a small farm in County Leitrim. He lived there with his wife Madeline for the rest of his life. It was important for him to be close to the land he knew as a child. In *Memoir*, he drew particular attention to walking through the small lanes with his mother and wrote,

> I am sure it is from those days I take the belief that the best of life is life lived quietly, where nothing happened but our calm journey through the day, where change is imperceptible and the precious life is everything.

He guarded his privacy, avoided most literary events and rarely gave readings of his work. He took his time writing, spent ten years on his final novel, *That They May Face the Rising Sun*. His reflections of the art and craft of writing were sparse but well thought out. 'I write because I need to write. I write to see. Through words I see.' He also said,

> As with most serious things, it begins with play, playing with sounds of words, their shape, their weight, their colour, their broken syllables; the fascination that the smallest change in any sentence altered all the words around it, and that they too had changed in turn. As in reading, when we become conscious that we are no longer reading romances or fables or adventures but versions of our own life, so it suddenly came to me that while I seemed to be play-

ing with words in reality I was playing with my own life. And words, for me, have always been presences as well as meanings. Through words I could experience my own life with more reality than ordinary living.

While McGahern childhood beliefs in a deity did not continue into adulthood, he could still call *The Barracks* 'not a novel but a religious poem', and could write to his friend Michael Laverty that 'all art approaches prayer'. A writer is first of all an artist. The artist/writer loves the world. Denis Sampson, who has written two books about McGahern said, 'the writer's business is to bring the reader through the outer layers of conventional reality into an experience of time and suffering which feels redemptive'. An instance of this appears later in Elizabeth's story when she is older, has returned to Ireland and illness threatens her life. This is how McGahern writes her story, redemptively addressing her pain and suffering.

> What is all this living and dying about anyway? [Old age, pain suffering, dying] weren't they so inevitable and obvious they were better ignored? Were the real problems faced and solved or declared insoluble or were they not simply lived in the changes of life? She could live her life though in its mystery, without any purpose, except to watch and bear witness. She did not care. She was alive and being was her ridiculous glory was well as her pain.

*

McGahern became one of the finest fiction writers in Ireland and has been compared to the greats he learned from – Chekhov, Yeats, Tolstoy. When the previously sacked primary school teacher died, dignitaries from all over Ireland queued up at his funeral to pay their respects. While John McGahern had living connections with other writers like Beckett and links across time with other great writers, his journey was more isolated than many. He ended up living in a quiet and remote part of Ireland, writing a few hours a day. He ran a small farm and found great enjoyment in meeting up in the local pub and chatting to his neighbours as well as attending events like cattle markets. But what internally sustained him, allowed his mind to return many times, which he did in his fiction, to his past? His past had many dark features, features that would have overcome someone without significant inner strength.

McGahern's father Sergeant McGahern was a complex presence. Into *The Dark*, *The Barracks*, and also in short stories like 'The Gold Watch', he made menacing entrances. And in McGahern's most well-known novel, *Amongst Women*, shortlisted for the Booker Prize, the brooding figure of Michael Moran has many characteristics of his father. Sergeant McGahern was a volatile man. John described his sudden changes in mood from charm and seduction to rage and beatings. There was, he said, a certain madness in his father and the picture painted is that of a psychopathic personality, totally devoid of empathy while behaving sadistically and then, when required switching on charm. When John was eight, he had impetigo and his face was covered in scabs. His father disinfected a sharp knife in boiling water, sat the boy down and proceeded to remove all the scabs with the knife.

John and his sisters endured regular beatings. John could not do much about it when he was a boy, and was less protected when his mother died. There came a day when it had to stop. Old enough and big enough, he took the situation in hand and laid down the law to his father. Enough! He'd had enough! Years later, when interviewed about it, he was asked what would have happened if his father had not listened and the beatings had continued. John said that he could have killed him.

John's mother was a deeply religious woman. She was central to an inner peace that he found early in life. Walking with her through country lanes and boreens, where speech was sparse and emotional togetherness profound, made an indelible impression on his mind. Throughout his life, he continued to re-find her in quietness.

When she died, the intensity, the enormity of what he struggled with leaps out and fills all space between the words. 'She was all that I had.'

Her loss to him was a damnation and he fought it as if it was about to engulf his soul. The world in Aughawillan, with her at its centre, collapsed and his boyish mind tried to call up the gods to come to his aid.

We can stand beside this ten-year-old boy and look around. The photo on the cover of *Memoir* allows this: he alone and expectant, in a field. With his mother gone, he moved to the barracks with his father and sisters. In time, he became the teenager who laid down the law to his father. He also became Elizabeth from *The Barracks*. Just as she found the little library in Aldgate East, he gained access to a neighbour's rich collection of books. This space and the space he entered into in his mind as he read was an escape. When the pain of reality was too much, he found solace.

And like Elizabeth, in books he found an in-between space. She'd felt the excitement with Halliday when she returned the books he had lent her, 'the first real books she'd been ever given and crying, "But they're real! They're not stories even. They're about my life."' He, sharing her wild delight said, 'All real lives are profoundly different and profoundly the same.' And John McGahern, among his books, found a window through which he could see out of his own world.

*

It's a long road for any writer to learn how to write about real lives. His reading provided solid ground upon which he grew as a person and a writer. I had another reason for presenting conversation between John and his mother in her sickbed. It is a window to look back again into the life of 'Patrick'. See what it lets us see. A boy's world. 'It is appointed unto men once to die and after that the judgement.' Hell, a stone's throw from heaven. A magical, mystical childhood in which the rituals of the church and the wind and rain intermingle. Where would John have turned to from a distant and abusive father if he had no mother to whom he could be attached and with whom he could share dreams?

The priest who raped 'Patrick', the priest who raped 'Brigit', Noel

Reynolds, Paul McGennis and others knew how to home in, to befriend, to groom for use as sexual objects, children such as this.

John could hold his mother's presence and her goodness inside him and build a productive life upon it. In many instances, the 'Patricks' and 'Brigits' did not, could not. So on top of the pain and shame, they are deprived of the opportunity to create a meaningful, satisfying and productive life.

In earlier chapters, I wrestled with the task of probing the mind of an abusive father and Father. This, as I indicated, is terrain upon which it is treacherous to walk. But I find it helpful to walk with John McGahern as he sought to understand the mind of his father, about whom, after his death, he had this to say.

> When word of my father's death reached me, the intensity of the conflicting emotions – grief, loss, relief – took me unawares. I believe the reaction was as much for those years in which his life and mine were entangled in a relationship neither of us wanted as for the man who had just met the death each of us face. He made many demands but gave little and always had to dominate. A life from which the past was so rigorously shut out had to be a life of darkness. Though I have more knowledge and experience of him than I have of any other person, I cannot say that I have fully understood him.

In my reckoning, it is never possible to fully understand someone who had no willingness, capacity or inclination to understand themselves. Heaney, in his interview with Denis O'Driscoll, said it well. The darkness does not hold formed words to simply produce when the time is right. The wish to search, the act of reaching in, the sense of what is found and the eyes and mind to look, must all be there, ready and willing. Inside some, the light of understanding never shines.

*

Who do you meet when you read a writer like McGahern? As I said, he was wary of literary events, especially where the event was billed as an opportunity to meet the 'real' writer. The Australian writer David Malouf echoed McGahern's sentiments when he said,

> People go to literary festivals thinking they are going to meet the real person, but they've already met the real person because the real person is in the writing. That's where you are freest, that's where you are more willing to go out on a limb and test yourself. It's the place where you make discoveries about yourself and surprise even you.

In a conversation between Hermione Lee and McGahern on April 2004, what was real was contrasted with the fashionable. Proust was quoted: 'Fashion which is begotten from a desire for change is quick to change itself.' Chekhov was mentioned: 'When a writer takes a pen into his or her hand, they accuse themselves of unanswerable egotism and all they can do with decency after that is to bow.'

> Each human being inhabits a private world which others can never fully know. If that human being is a writer they write out of that world. If that human being is a reader they read out of that world. The difference between the two is that the writer has the capacity (and sometimes the misfortune) to dramatise that world. For the reader to have a spiritual gain, he or she must give generously of themselves in the act of reading.

And extending James Joyce's description of a piano as a coffin of notes requiring a player, John McGahern believed the book to be a coffin of words. 'It won't,' he said, 'live again until a reader brings it to life, and it will emerge in as many different versions as the readers it's honoured enough to find.'

12

To Infinity; and Beyond

I have said above that craft and care are called for if we are to engage with spirituality and 'God'. I likened it to traversing a snow-capped mountain range, where you might at any moment trigger an avalanche. In Italy a few centuries ago, you could be burned alive if you deviated from accepted church teaching and nowadays (April 2019) in Brunei, a Muslim who renounces their belief in Islam can be stoned to death.

In the West, debate about God between believers and non-believers can be very fractious. An example of an unsatisfactory debate was on the Australian Broadcasting Corporation's *Q and A* programme in 2014. There were two panellists, Richard Dawkins, an outspoken atheist and Cardinal George Pell, then head of the Catholic church in Australia. For an hour, they took questions and debated, although it was not so much a debate as an example of the irresistible force meeting the unmovable object, or two old gladiators slugging it out in a coliseum. While neither was the victor, each saw themselves as superior to the other. Both were convinced that they possessed the truth and the other was in error.

Paul Tillich challenged his fellow theologians when he wrote,

> We can no longer speak of God easily to anybody because he will immediately question: 'Does God exist?' Now the very asking of that question signifies that the symbols of God have become meaningless. For God, in the question, has become one of the innumerable objects in time and space which may or may not exist. And this is not the meaning of God at all.

Two thousand five hundred years ago in Athens, a man who had heard about Socrates's reputation asked to be taught. Socrates refused. Instead, he offered an experience of thinking. The debates Socrates facilitated were not conducted to lead to a victor and a vanquished, to one being in truth and the other error. Philosophy – *philo-sophia* – is the love of wisdom/knowledge. In such a loving search, you may wander into the space of abstract thought, but do not remain there or elevate such space above where the ordinary and everyday is lived. You come to 'know' justice by living a just life.

In a globalised world, where is the space to love wisdom and knowledge? How do we create the conditions for a debate about God and religion? Some commentators on the world stage have hoped that the question of God and religion would fade away. Man in his rational maturity would have no need for them. This was Nietzsche's expectation and today Stephen Pinker has expressed a similar hope.

Yet somehow, God and religion have not gone away and we must continue with the debate, one that must be engaged in without superiority.

I begin with Freud and Oskar Pfister. Pfister was a good friend of Freud and his family. He was a Lutheran pastor and practised psychoanalysis in Zurich. Pfister first visited Freud in 1909 and gave him a give of a little silver model of the Matterhorn. Referring to the gift in a subsequent letter, Freud wrote, 'It reminds me of a remarkable man who came to see me one day, a true servant of God, a man in the very idea of whom I should have had difficulty in believing, in that he feels the need to do spiritual good to everyone he meets.'

Freud was clear that he had no belief in a God and outlined his thoughts in *The Future of an Illusion*. Freud's thinking is briefly summarised as follows.

There is a fundamental antagonism between 'Humans' and 'Nature'. Nature is out to destroy man by fire, flood, disease. Man is helpless and faces continuous anxiety about his survival and well being. What can man do? He has 'been here before'. In other words, there is an infantile prototype. The helpless child fears and needs the father's protection. He sees the same issue when faced with 'Nature'. He makes gods to avoid living in constant anxiety. When religions arise, they also offer a solution to the shortcoming of civilisation where injustice and inequality exist. Morality and issues of fairness, justice, love et cetera become subsumed inside religious beliefs.

Freud also said that an understanding of religions, and their histories, was a necessary part of engagement with the world. People like Dawkins and Pinker do not see an engagement with the world of religion as necessary or useful. I think an engagement with religion and religious belief is not just useful but an urgent necessity in our times.

Before the publication of *The Future of an Illusion*, Freud had concerns about its effect on his friend. He wrote to him in October 1927. In the letter, he said,

> I wanted to write it for a long time, and postponed it out of regards for you, but the impulse became to strong. The subject matter – as you will easily guess – is my completely negative attitude to religion, in any form and however attenuated, and, through there can be nothing new to you in this, I feared, and still fear, that such a public profession of my attitude will be painful to you. When you have read it you must let me know what measure of toleration and understanding you are able to preserve for this hopeless pagan.
> Always your cordially devoted Freud.

Five days later Pfister replied.

> … As for your anti-religious pamphlet, there is nothing new to me in your rejection of religion. I look forward to it with pleasurable anticipation. A powerful-minded opponent of religion is certainly of more service to it than a thousand useless supporters. In music, philosophy, and religion I go different ways to you… I have always believed that every man should state his honest opinion aloud and plainly. You have always been tolerant towards me, and am I to be intolerant of your atheism?

In his correspondence, Pfister indicated his intention to write a reply to Freud's *The Future of an Illusion*. Freud replied the following day.

Such is your magnanimity that I expected no other answer to my 'declaration of war'. The prospect of your making a public stand against my pamphlet gives me positive pleasure, it will be refreshing in the discordant critical chorus for which I am prepared. We know that by different routes we aspire to the same objectives for poor humanity.

Pfister's reply, called *The Illusion of a Future*, appeared the following year (although it was not published in English until 1993). To briefly summarise Pfister. He questioned Freud's reliance on 'science' as the key to human progress. Such reliance is an illusion. Music, philosophy and religion were to Freud problematic or of little importance. Pfister critiqued Freud's narrow scientism. He regarded Freud's attitude to philosophy as simplistic and his knowledge of religions inadequate. Religions and religious belief and practice had great variety. The reasons why people were religious were numerous. To equate faith with childish wishes was simplistic. Jesus was a figure with an internal world where freedom was central.

Science, Pfister states, is not pure and not always residing in the objective. He outlined how science used and depended upon many 'unscientific' attributes to get to its discoveries. Dreams and imagination and intuition were frequently present in the mind of the innovator. Many things are known by intuition and through non-scientific methods that later are proved to be scientifically correct.

*

Freud also sent a copy of *The Future of an Illusion* to Romain Rolland. Rolland (1866–1944) had won the Nobel Prize for Literature in 1915. He was brought up a Catholic but turned away from the church and accused it of fermenting World War I and, once the war had started, doing nothing to bring it to an end. He was outspoken about anti-Semitism and at that time was called 'the conscience of Europe'. Disillusioned with Western constrictions, Rolland turned to the East to find more space for thought. When Freud wrote to Rolland in 1926, he said,

I revered you as an artist and apostle of love for mankind many years before I knew you. I myself have always advocated the love of mankind not out of sentimentality or idealism but for sober, economic reasons: because in the face of our instinctual drives and the world as it is I was compelled to consider this love as indispensable for the preservation of the human species as say, technology.

When Rolland wrote back, Freud replied, 'That I have been allowed to exchange a greeting with you will remain a happy memory to the end of my days.'

On reading *The Future of an Illusion*, Rolland believed that Freud had paid insufficient attention to 'the oceanic feeling'. This was a psychological term coined by Rolland. It is a feeling of limitlessness. According to Rolland's definition, this feeling is the source of all religious energy which permeates the various religious systems. It is a sensation of an indissoluble bond, as of being connected with the external world in its integral form. This feeling is an entirely subjective fact and is not an article of faith. Rolland's view was that one may justifiably call oneself religious on the basis of this oceanic feeling alone. Freud took Rolland's views and the term oceanic feeling seriously and later incorporated them in his book *Civilisation and its Discontents*.

*

One psychoanalyst who has seriously engaged with religion is Neville Symington. He distinguished between revealed religion and natural religion. He is interested in the psychological implications of each. In a revealed religion, an omnipotent and omniscient god overpowers parts of the self. Natural religion arises out of ontological reflection. Being and the essence of being are central to ontology. What is of fundamental significance is existence itself. The fact that a world exists, that we exist, is a profound mystery. On another level, Symington is concerned about the split between psychoanalysis and religion. Jon Stokes, in the foreword to Symington's *Emotion and Spirit* wrote that

Neville Symington makes the case that both traditional religion and psychoanalysis are failing because they exist apart and do not incorporate each other's values. Religion needs psychoanalysis so that it can become more relevant to people's emotional lives and their most intimate relationships. Psychoanalysis needs religion so that it can contain those core spiritual values which give life meaning. Symington emphasises the relationship between the moral dimension of the mind and the emotional and spiritual health of the individual.

*

Hans Loewald, who I introduced in an earlier chapter, has also engaged with religion. In *Reflections on Religious Experience,* a paper given at Yale in 1974 to promote scholarly exchange between psychoanalysis and the humanities, he said, 'I hope it may lead a step beyond what psychoanalysis has contributed so far to the understanding and misunderstanding of religion.'

To give a summary of Loewald's line of thought: the early years and stages of a human life remain a living source, a well from which we draw sustenance all our life and which provides the raw materials of creativity. The emergence of a consciousness, of a mind, of intellectual and reasoning faculties does not ever turn its back on the first building blocks out of which that mind was constructed. If it does, it becomes sterile and destructive of life.

Loewald believed Freud overvalued later powers and tended to commit earlier powers to the realm of illusion and escape from reality. Loewald, on the other hand, gave increased importance to earlier phases and their continued place as a source of creativity. The past is a living past; an infant 'lost in time' is not immature; ecstatic absorption in the abiding present, the *nunc stans,* is not a denial of time passing, but an appreciation of eternity, of the dissolution of past, present and future. Like Rolland, Loewald saw strands of Western thought as dominated by a narrow scientism. This scientism diminished that which does not operate within its orbit. Intimations of eternity put us in touch with earlier and still active levels of our being. The world and its understanding is not exclusively the province of rationality.

*

In 1930, Ella Sharpe (who has been referred to and will feature in the next chapter) wrote about the discovery of the cave paintings at Altamira, northern Spain, in 1879. These drawings were believed to be 17,000 years old – the (then) oldest known examples of human art. Excavations revealed that the artists lived in the outer part of the cave, but went into deeper and more inaccessible parts in order to create their drawings by the light of a lamp. The paintings consisted of a number of bison and other animals, which were depicted realistically and in bright colours. The cave also contained drawings of men as hunters and men wearing animal masks. Dancing was depicted. The masked and unmasked men danced in procession around a slain bison. Sharpe wrote,

> ...great art is a self-preservative functioning. A vital communication is made to us in picture, statue, drama, novel. It is life that is danced, a world that is built in music. When these things are supreme, are perfection, we rest satisfied in contemplation. From a world of apprehension and anxiety, a world of temporal things, of vicissitudes and death, we temporarily escape. In those few moments of conviction, immortality is ours.

*

Karen Armstrong was a Catholic nun in the late 1950s and early 60s. The order she belonged to prided obedience. If your superior instructed you to plant the cabbage plants upside down, it was expected you do so without question, indeed without thought. The will of your superior was the will of God. Your will was nothing. Perfect sanctity was total obedience. After seven years, Armstrong left the convent and was determined to remove herself as far as possible from organised religion. Years later, after time spent in the study of literature and working for the BBC on some religious affairs programmes, she returned to study and to understand religion and today is regarded as an international scholar in the field. She has written numerous books. Her speech on compassion was the 2008 TED talk of the year.

In her book *The Case for God*, Armstrong explores the life of the Neolithic in 9000 BC. Just as Hans Loewald explored religious experience as part of the formative influence in the development of the human being, Armstrong examined the place of religious experience in the group life of the Neolithic as evidenced in the cave paintings of Lascaux in Southern France. Humans began to paint in the caves of Lascaux around 9000 BC. As at Altamira, these caves are not easily accessible and people used oil lamps and crawled to the deepest parts of the cave system. Armstrong asked why did they do this and her answer was, a desire to cultivate a sense of the transcendent. She argues, 'The desire to cultivate a sense of the transcendent may be the defying human characteristic.' When humans began to paint in the caves of Lascaux, they turned their minds to Being, to Spirit, to All. The ultimate reality was not a personalised God, but a transcendent mystery that could never be plumbed. In line with Rolland and Loewald, she claims that if we confine the painters of Altimira and Lascaux to 'a primitive' stage of human development, we have lost something important. Armstrong stated,

> human beings are spiritual animals. Indeed, there is a case or arguing that Homo sapiens is also *Homo religiosus*. Men and women... created religions at the same time as they created works of art. This was not simply because they wanted to propitiate powerful forces but these early faiths expressed the wonder and mystery that seems always to have been an essential component of the human experience of this beautiful and terrifying world... Like art, religion has been an attempt to find meaning and value in life.

In India in the Vedic religious tradition during the tenth century, the Brahman was the whole of reality, the essence of all existence, 'The All'. It was Being itself, the totality of the cosmos, all life animate and inanimate, the power that binds everything. A ritual called the Brahmodya sought to place human beings as close as possible to the Brahman. It was a communal activity. To prepare, people fasted and spent time in private thought. Then they formally assembled and spoke together. They were aiming to find the most appropriate words to capture a sense of the transcendent, to push language to its limits and beyond and place the community in the presence of the Brahman, the Divine.

A person spoke and tried with their words to express what the transcendent meant to them. Another would respond. I expect poetry was used, and song. There was discussion as to who spoke best. The one of lesser words withdrew. A third person contributed. Discussion followed. This process carried on, sometimes for days. Eventually, only one was left, one set of words that were better than all others at conjuring up the ineffable. However, it was not those words that were considered the summit of achievement. It was in that silence that the Brahman was most present.

In her study of religions, Armstrong emphasises the fact that an organised religion is a communal entity and religious practices serve to bring a community together. And that in the collective, what is most important is how people threat each other. The crucial test that needs to be applied to any religion is the presence of compassion.

She also explores the nature of belief. 'To believe' used to mean, literally translated, 'to hold dear'. Armstrong shows how in 1277 students of theology had first to study science and then they began to view God through the mental categories that they had become familiar with. She says that this type of reduction occurred in the Christian church in the Middle Ages and they forgot that 'Aristotle had insisted that each field of study had its own rationale and that it was dangerous to apply the rules and methods of one science to another.'

Another backwards step came with the reformation and the Council of Trent. Difference between different types of Christians had to be defined. Exactitude crept in and Rome and the pope became centres of power. When people can't truly respect difference, they regress to fundamentalism. And, as history shows, once you believe that an omnipotent god is on your side, you can justify the most horrific atrocities.

*

Thus far, I have done no more than set down a few markers that in Socratic tradition might provide a starting point for debate. While I have only touched on a few strands of thought, what I have done serves my present purpose, which is to establish a piece of ground upon which to think.

And as I stand on my piece of ground, in the presence of those whose views I have summarised, I can look out at vast continents of thought. I see many monuments to gods: the Egyptian pyramids, the Dome of St Peters, the Al-Aqsa mosque in Jerusalem, the reclining Buddha in Bangkok and many others. But if I really imagine myself on that piece of ground, it is not long before I am disturbed. People are heading my way. While they are still at a distance, I shut my eyes and recall Hazlitt's words: 'The spirit of philosophy consists in the ability to think and the patience to wait for a result.' When they come near, I will need all the patience I can muster.

The first to arrive is a man in a long black robe. He won't place his feet on my piece of land but stops at the edge. He tells me that I was baptised into the One Holy Roman Catholic and Apostolic church. I belong to them. Once a catholic, always a catholic. He chides my laxness and tells me the arms of mother church are always open for the return of the prodigal. When I say I lost faith in his doctrines, he smiles sadly and turns away. I think he mutters something about earlier times when the likes of me would have been excommunicated. Was that an expression of concern for my good or the gimlet eye of the canon lawyer doing a soul count?

But his departing words are drowned out by song. I am visited by a singing group. From a distance, they looked like flower people from the 1960s but now I am surrounded by a group of born-again Christians. Filled to overflowing with joy and goodness, they promise salvation. When I describe what they are standing on, their interest wanes and they glance at my ground as if it was barren. I reach to my library shelf to offer them something to read. They hold the Bible high; with eyes on paradise, they turn their back and troop away.

Although relieved, I soon regret their departure because they have been replaced by an ominous presence. Sword-wielding men praise their god and want to cut my head off. In their eyes, I am an infidel and somehow the spilling of my blood is explained as an act of homage. Centuries ago, they were called crusaders. No problem killing in a good cause. This present group praise their prophet. I try to talk to them. I tell them that at the time of Mohammad's death in 632, no one was forced to convert and that in the year 700 conversion was forbidden by law. Other groups that lived alongside Muslims, Jews and Christians were granted religious liberty as protected minorities. They know nothing of such history. They quote Sharia law. They seem unaware that Sharia law was only written down in the eighth and ninth centuries. It was formulated when people began to write about the daily practices of Mohammad; the way he spoke, greeted other, how he ate, washed and worshipped. Mohammad had fully and perfectly surrendered himself to God. If you model yourself on the prophet, act as he acted, you may also develop an interior receptiveness to God. The laws in themselves meant nothing. They were means to an end. The aim was to develop a sense of God's presence in everyday events, in the here-and-now. A 'Muslim' is literally 'one whose life bows to the Creator, to al-Lah'.

But history and its truth means nothing to them.

My final visitors do not carry weapons but for reasons that at first are not clear they are enraged with me. They mock my piece of ground. Any mention of God, religion, church provokes them. They speak of Richard Dawkins, Christopher Hitchens, A.C. Grayling. Some of them demand I answer the question Paul Tillich deemed unanswerable. Some of these people seem intent on dislodging me. There is a tone of pity expressed, sadness even, that I can't join them in their certainty. They have an absolute belief about their views and, if pressed, are obliged to admit that I am entitled to mine, although they give no indication that they will actually listen to anything I say or respect the ground I stand upon. Science is their god, their faith absolute.

*

My 'piece of ground' is a place in the kingdom of my mind. My piece of ground, this room in my mind, is where past and present live side by side, where the thinking of poetry and the thinking of science and thinking of spirituality are at ease with each other.

In Goethe's *Faust*, we are told a story of man who knows everything and nothing. His predicament, in his words,

> Philosophy have I digested,
> The whole of law and Medicine,
> From each its secrets I have wrested,
> Theology, alas, thrown in.
> Poor fool, with all this sweated lore,
> I stand no wiser than I was before.

Faust's story is like a road movie. A person begins a journey propelled by an absence within. Faust finds himself, at the end of his journey, after his epic wanderings, working a piece of ground, a place on earth that is reclaimed from the sea.

*

Preoccupation with defending your position can make you think you are alone, but I am not some lonely isolated soul and this piece of ground is not just inhabited by those here mentioned. There are men and women who profess faith, belong to a church and find within it a spiritual life. Others no longer belong to a church or religious group but have retained a sense of gratitude for the experience their church provided them with, a sense of awe and wonder at the world, and a deep appreciation of the need to be part of a community have proved sustaining. There are others whom churches have severely damaged. Having offered access to the awe and wonder of creation, they provided instead a hell on earth.

There are those who have never belonged to any church or recognised religion. Some faces are famous, others unknown. They are a strange collection. Some are long dead. This does not surprise me as for some time I have held the belief that the dead can be more alive than the living, their vitality eternally perpetuated in their writing or their art. And the one feature that is common to each and every one is that they uphold the spirit of the Brahmodya. One way or another, privately and publicly that spirit enriches their lives.

The cave painters of Lascaux and Altimira are alongside those who designed the great monuments and created art that speaks of life beyond. Shakespeare is here and John Keats. The list is long. Heaney, McGahern, Hazlitt, Emily Dickinson speak to me and for me. All unafraid to tilt at windmills, to tackle things larger than themselves with courage and hope. And they know when to pull back; where their limitations are. And Plato, who is among them, wrote,

> Concerning these things [ultimate truth] there is not, nor will there be, any treatise written by me. For they do not at all admit of being expounded in writing, as do objects of other (scientific) studies… only after long, arduous conversance with the matter itself…a light suddenly breaks upon the soul as from a kindled flame, and once born keeps alive of itself…only to a few men is the exposition of these things of any profit, and they only need a slight indication of them for their discovery.

There is another feature about life and knowledge that is common to this group. They are conscious that time has many dimensions. While humans in one sense have a long history on this planet, in a grander scheme of things they play a very minor part. On a twenty-four-hour time frame, with the Big Bang happening at midnight, humans in some primitive from appeared twenty-three hours and fifty-six minutes later, at four minutes to midnight. In the grand scheme of things, we have not been around very long as reflecting, thinking beings.

I am aware that those thinkers I have already mentioned are a tiny group among a multitude; countless thinkers through the ages have addressed 'the sacred subjects'. And I refer not only to those who declare their interest in religious thought and culture; many philosophers and artists have turned their attention this way. Many times, I have been dwarfed by the magnitude of what there is to read. It is like setting out on what you think is a challenging hillside walk only to find yourself in the midst of vast mountains that intimidate and look unclimbable. Time to pause and ask a simple question: what do I believe, remembering that the old meaning of 'I believe' is 'I hold dear'.

I believe, along with Hans Loewald, that our past is a living past and to get lost in time is not infantile immaturity; to be ecstatically absorbed in the abiding present, the *nunc stans,* is not a denial of time passing, but an appreciation of eternity, which is (unlike what is everlasting) a dissolution of past, present and future.

Charles Morgan captures a sense of childlike wonder and the abiding present in his beautiful essay entitled 'The Word "Serenity"'.

> Have you ever watched a child, in the full activity of childhood, halt as though an invisible hand had touched his shoulder, and stare? I remember such occasions in my own childhood, and in my manhood also, when a thing seen, which a moment ago was one of many and of no particular significance, has become singular, has separated itself from the stream of consciousness, and has become not an object but a source. What is the child staring at? Not at the flower or the drop of water or the face. The thing seen, which ordinarily halts our observation, has become not a wall but a window. The opaque has become the serene; he is looking through it, through the disparate appearances of life, which we falsely call re-

ality, towards the origin of that light by which all things are seen. What awes the child is not that he has arrived at an intellectual understanding of the order of things but that he has perceived that there is an order of things... An artist is a child who stares, not at the imprisoning walls of life, but outward through the window.

I believe that great fiction writing has a spiritual quality and poetry in particular is a constant window-maker. Poetry is deeply interested in the ordinary and the everyday and respects other ways of looking. It respects Kant's wisdom when he said, 'Intuition without concept is blind; concept without intuition is empty.' A more poetic rendition of the same sentiments came from the pen of Kahill Gibran: 'Reason and imagination are the rudder and the sails that guide the soul through life.'

I believe that our deepest experiences are beyond words. Music, image and song are like Gibran's sails, without which our life can get stuck. I labour with poetry to capture music, image and song, to create and cultivate my piece of ground and hopefully assist others to do likewise.

The Victorian photographer Julia Margaret Cameron described how she went about her work. She said,

> when focusing and coming to something which to my eye was very beautiful, I stopped there instead of screwing the lens to a more definite focus which all other photographers insist upon.

I think beauty, the infinite, what is beyond, is best appreciated by not screwing the lens of our mind. A little poem can be a big thing. Charles Simic said poetry is like philosophy because it can capture enormously complex matters in a few words. Like philosophy, poetry is concerned with Being. What is a lyric poem, he asks, 'but the recreation of the experience of Being. [It says] the unsayable and lets the truth of Being shine through.' This echoes what Symington and Wittgenstein said: the fact that a world exists, that we exist, is the profound mystery. 'It is not HOW things are in the world that is mystical, but *that* it exists.'

I believe individually and collectively we need to find our piece of ground that is both private and common. Compassion is not a moral choice; it is a necessity thrust upon us because of our fundamental need and dependence upon each other. Compassion is intrinsically linked to suffering. Compassion makes you a connoisseur of suffering, or we could say conversely that it is only through having suffered that a person can know how another has suffered. As John Keats said, we create our own souls by the way we live a life and develop a mind.

To paraphrase Shakespeare, poetry imaginatively bodies forth and offers forms to things unknown, turns them to shape, and gives to airy nothing a local habitation and a name. Even if the poet's eye rolls in a fine frenzy, the poet manages to steer a path between the lunatic and the obsessed lover. When he/she speaks – as the Greeks said – it is the language of the gods.

Maybe the gods are closer than we think!

Are We There Yet?

He owned his own church. It was small –
like St Kevin's at Glendalough in County Wicklow
Ireland or the church of San Carlos Borroméo
at Carmel in Monterey County California –

and it was very beautiful. It wasn't real, of course.
No. It was complete in his mind,
so he could take it with him
all the time, wherever he went.

He would slip away when he was with you,
you never noticed because
when you talked and he listened
he gave his full attention.

And only later, after he'd gone
did you know he had quietly
taken you there, and the two of you
had stood together in silent prayer.

I believe that a love of literature can be a window, a portal that allows entry into a transcendent universe. In his memoir, the Irish writer Denis Sampson wrote, 'My love of literature had become my deepest faith, for in it I had found the knowledge that gives imaginative depth to life.' And in the 1986 T.S. Eliot Memorial Lectures, Seamus Heaney said poetry has a special status among the literary arts, that 'the poet is credited with a power to open unexpected and unedited communications between our nature and the nature of the reality we inhabit'.

Of the true poem, Robert Frost said,

> Read a hundred times it can never lose its sense of a meaning that once unfolded by surprise as it went. It begins in delight, it inclines to the impulse, it assumes direction with the first line laid down, it runs a course of lucky events and ends in a clarification of life - not necessarily a great clarification, such as sects and cults are founded on, but in a momentary stay against confusion.

A momentary stay.

Zero?

Zero is nought. Nothing from nothing springs.
What's made must have its maker, effect its cause,
Yet who can say from where creation sings?

We live by physics' laws, are drawn by nature's strings,
Science fiction's fiction – the grown-up's Santa Claus.
Zero is nought. Nothing from nothing springs.

The last in line digs deep and sprints and wins,
Is first to touch the tape to loud applause,
Now who can say from where creation sings?

To certainty in science mankind sternly clings,
Seeks sameness in what will be, what is and was.
Zero is nought. Nothing from nothing springs.

A poem comes from nought, from zero grows its wings.
Be brave, be swept into its slipstream because
You may learn from where creation sings?

On science's fertile ground do not fear the slings
Of wild imaginings. Become a wizard of Oz!
Zero is nought? Nothing from nothing springs?
Will you say from where creation sings?

13

Living the Dream

It is a strange fact that many who claim to be 'living the dream' are creating their own nightmare. They exist in a constant state of reaction while awake, have no time to rest and don't know how to respond. Habituated to a heightened state of mental alertness, the rhythms of the brain lose synchronicity, and sleep, which by its nature should re-establish those rhymes, is disrupted.

Monitors were worn by 91,000 people to study their circadian rhythms in a study published in 2018 in *The Lancet Psychiatry*. Failure to separate oneself from the stimulus of a mobile phone or other electronic devices when rest was required at night can cause, or significantly contribute to, poorer mental health.

When we sleep, we dream. We may not remember the dream, but it happens and a wearable monitor can tell us when and for how long. A good night is necessary for a good day. But a good night can also prefigure a creative day.

Many thinkers recognised the place sleep and the dream have in unlocking creative forces within the mind. Dmitri Mendeleev discovered the periodic table in a dream. He had struggled to logically organise the chemical elements. He wrote each element on a card but could not think of how they should be ordered. He fell asleep at his desk and woke and, 'In a dream I saw a table where all the elements fell into place as required.'

August Kekule struggled to understand how atoms in benzene were arranged. He dozed in a chair in front of the fire and dreamt of atoms in the shape of a snake. He woke and saw that benzene molecules were made up of rings of carbon atoms.

Descartes said the four rules of scientific progress that are the basis of scientific method came to him in a dream.

Otto Loewi, the father of neuroscience, who won the Nobel Prize in 1936, had puzzled over the way nerve signals in the brain were transmitted. After seventeen years of pondering, he had a pair of similar dreams on successive nights which showed him they were caused by chemical transmission.

Niels Bohr said a dream led him to discover the structure of the atom. He saw a nucleus surrounded by spinning electrons.

Albert Einstein dreamed he was careering down a steep mountainside so fast the stars changed in appearance. On waking, he formulated his famous theory.

*

In his book *A Terrible Beauty*, the historian Peter Watson began his exploration of the twentieth century by examining five events that occurred in the year 1900. On 25 October, Pablo Picasso arrived in Paris. Also in October, the physicist Max Planck, who was exploring electromagnetic radiation, send a postcard to a colleague Heinrich Rubens. On the postcard, he wrote an equation suggesting energy was emitted in pulses and not continuously. Quantum physics was born. Planck gave a paper to the Berlin Physics Society. Because for the previous twenty years he had proposed so many theories that were wrong, his presentation on that occasion was followed by a polite silence and no questions were asked. In March, Arthur Evans, a British archaeologist, landed at Heraklion on the northern coastline of Crete. He had spent years trying to buy the site at Knossos. He set to work and within days he and his team of thirty found something which would keep him there for the next twenty-five years, namely evidence of a civilisation that predated ancient Rome and Greece. The Minoan civilisation dated from

2500 to 1500 BC. Homer's *Odyssey* and Odysseus and his companions were not simply fictitious characters. Later in the same month (24 March), Hugo de Vries, a Dutch botanist, read a paper in Mannheim called 'The Law of Segregation of Hybrids'. He identified what later became known as genes. On 6 January, a review of Freud's *The Interpretation of Dreams* was published.

Freud put dreams on the map in a new way. The dream is an entry point into the mind: to learn how the dream works is to become knowledgeable about the workings of the mind. Dreams do more than attend to puzzles external to ourselves; they offer new ways to see and know ourselves.

Freud continued to write until his death in 1939 but he never wavered in his belief that *The Interpretation of Dreams* was his most significant piece of work and, as he said, 'it contains…the most valuable of all the discoveries it has been my good fortune to make. Insight such as this falls to one's lot but one in a lifetime'. The book was not a runaway publishing success and in the first ten years only sold five hundred copies. But some people were intrigued. In 1905, a surgeon in London called Wilfred Trotter told his brother-in-law Ernest Jones about a doctor in Vienna who listened to *everything* his patients told him. Trotter and Jones learned German so they could read Freud's writings. Meanwhile, in the midst of other great shifts in the world, the doctor in Vienna continued to examine his own dreaming mind and the dreaming minds of his patients.

Freud was not the first on the scene. The dream had intrigued humans for a long time, intrigued and frightened us. When Freud died, W.H. Auden wrote a poem, 'In Memory of Sigmund Freud', in which these words appear:

> But he would have us remember most of all
> To be enthusiastic over the night
> Not only for the sense of wonder
> It alone has to offer, but also
> Because it needs our love.

*

While Trotter and Jones (who became a leading figure in taking Freud's thought to the English-speaking world) studied German and read the writings of the doctor in Vienna, Freud employed a young man called Otto Rank as his secretary. Rank learned from Freud but soon Freud was learning from Rank. Rank had an extensive knowledge of art and culture. He had a particular interest in myths and poetry and, through his contact with Freud and his circle, was stimulated to explore the relationship of dreams to myths and poetry. Writing about dreams and poetry, Rank said,

> Since time immemorial men have noticed that their nocturnal dream-productions reveal various similarities to the creations of poetry. Poets and thinkers have shown a predilection to trace those relationships as evident in form, content and effect... The dream researcher will be interested in these points: in the appreciation and the understanding which the intuitive experts of the psyche had for the riddle of the dream; in the way in which the poets have used the knowledge of the dream-life in their works; and finally in the deeper connections which may be recognised between the strange capacities of the 'sleeping' psyche and the 'inspired' one. Most of all the psychoanalyst will be satisfied to learn that men of genius in their intuitive comprehension have always found in the dreams a meaning.

Rank compiled an itemised list of poets and philosophers who not only believed dreams were meaningful but that they occupied a special place in human understanding. The poet Hebbel writing in 1838 had said, 'the human psyche is a miraculous being, and the central point of all its secrets is the dream'. Other examples – Tolstoy: 'When I am awake, I may deceive myself about myself, the dream however gives me the right gauge by which to measure the level of moral perfection which I have reached.' The philosopher Lichtenberg: 'The dream is a life which, put together with ours, becomes what we call human life. The dreams lose themselves gradually into our waking, and one cannot say when one starts and the other ceases.' Nietzsche: 'The habituations of our dreams hold us by a string in broad daylight and even in the most serene moments of our awake mind.' The list continues and includes references to Dryden, Shakespeare, Chaucer, Byron, Milton and Dickens.

In 1914, a fourth German edition of *The Interpretation of Dreams* appeared with two extra chapters, written not by Freud but by Rank. The chapters are called 'Dream and Poetry' and 'Dreams and Myths'. Also in 1914, Freud considered completely rewriting *The Interpretation of Dreams,* a joint publication with Rank as co-writer. Rank was one of the first people who began to erect something new upon the foundations which Freud had constructed.

*

Many others would continue to build. Thinkers of many persuasions and artists of many forms found in dreams and in conversations about dreaming, a rich source of creativity and sustainability. Their minds and capacity to think enlarged. They found in their dreams a daily well of refreshment. For some, it was like going for a morning walk; for others, like the time of day they put aside for meditation. The dream you have is totally outside your control and therefore offers a regular lesson in humility. It also grounds you in experience. You may come up with some grand theory about your dream, but if you haven't attended to the actual emotional experience which the having of the dream brings, you'll get nowhere.

In this book, in my argument, dreaming is a form of thinking. Before I continue looking at others in the past hundred years who also built upon Freud's foundations, I will give a reason why I think people are drawn to dreams.

In a dream, you can be in two places at once. You are in a room with the door closed but you are also seeing through the closed door. In a dream, you can be in the present and at the same time be in the past. You are adult and child. You can be on opposite sides of the world, in Sydney and London at the same time.

In a dream, you can be yourself and someone else. You can see a face which is a composite of two people that you know. In a dream, two parts of your own mind can talk to each other as if they were separate people.

In a dream, you can do the impossible. In a dream, you can be the impossible.

*

When Ella Sharpe became a psychoanalyst in London in 1921 it was said of her that she knew her Shakespeare as a good preacher knows his Bible. She had taught English literature for twenty years and in blending her literary mind with her psychoanalytic mind she constructed something original on Freud's foundations. She came from a working-class area of England and some have wondered why she made her way to London in 1917 to study Freud. Her interest in literature, especially drama and poetry, is a partial answer. But I think she was responding to the offer of something new. It wasn't just new knowledge, but an opportunity to enlarge her mind and use it in a new way. This wasn't just an age when more people were looking for greater social and political freedom; it wasn't just an age when women were campaigning for the right to vote; they were open to the possibilities of a liberation of their minds.

I have already quoted Ella Sharpe in the chapter on Freud, a piece written just before she died in 1947. Reflecting on her work, she said,

> I experience a rich variety of living through my work. I contact all sorts and kinds of living, all imaginable circumstances, human tragedy and human comedy, humour and dourness, the pathos of the defeated, the incredible endurances and victories that some souls achieve over human fate.

And I have mentioned her comments on the cave paintings in Altimira, when she said, 'It is *life* that is danced, a world that is built in music.'

So, when Sharpe decided a write a book on dreams, we would expect something new. In 1937, she published *Dream Analysis*. There she said that dreams make use of the poetic diction of lyric poetry. The language of poetry is evocative because it can use many devices like simile, metaphor, alliteration, onomatopoeia. Sharpe's ear would have heard the sound of *ghaoth*. She would have made her journey to Salamanca. To hearing a dream, she brought her poetry-attuned mind.

Imagine a poet who stands before the cave paintings of Altimira. He carried a light to help him find his way. As he sees through the lambent flame, he looks for words, for language, that will lift the image from the wall and allow him to take it with him to the outside world.

On Freud's foundations, Sharpe constructed something that might be called a poetic art gallery. Although Freud productively spent time thinking as a poet, he sometimes was uneasy lingering in that space and when Havelock Ellis praised him for his artistic qualities, Freud took offence. Such a compliment he said was 'the most refined and amicable form of resistance, calling me a great artist in order to injure the validity of our scientific claims'.

I suspect Sharpe would have gracefully accepted such praise without fearing her claim to be a systematic thinker would be diminished. She was happy to make a comparison between dreams and works of art. We find her referring to 'the picture on the dream-canvas' and paying very close attention to words, listening not just for their intended meaning but to their poetry. The dream is a psychic work of art and dreaming is a creative activity. Vision and voice in the dream are not just expressions but transformative activities. Language not just in its meaning but also in its music explores, remembers, evokes, represents, explains, transforms and communicates. All usages of language are important but a poetic way of speaking is a particularly rich area of investigation. Poems are constructed in a certain manner. They intend to evoke the reader's response. But poems are written not just to be read, but to be spoken aloud. They need to be heard. A poem is a communication between different people. At the same time, it is a communication between different parts of the self.

*

Rest is a profound human need. Sleep is an absolute necessity. With sleeping and dreaming, the rhythms of our brain can be so disrupted we will go insane. Forced sleep deprivation is a recognised form of torture.

If you live to the age of ninety you will spend twenty-five to thirty years asleep.

It is a common experience of the dreamer that the dream has undefined edges or borders. When we watch a film on screen, it begins with a name and ends with a list of credits. Even if at the outer borders of our dream we see signposts that enable us to travel beyond the dream and into the rest of our life, our past, our present or our future, the night, the darkness or dimness beckons. In other words, the dream has no specific stating point nor a specified destination. It is an unpunctuated fragment. The place where we arrive is a place to rest. Soon we will be on the move again. There is always more to find out. What remains to be known is unrestricted.

Three is another aspect to the movement of dreams. Many people have recognised and written about it. It is that 'dreaming' is not only a nocturnal event. 'Dreaming' occurs outside sleep. Our brain, like our heart, is always in motion. Our unconscious is always in motion. Here the whole meaning of dreaming is extended or the arc of the dream is broadened. Glen Gabbard and Thomas Ogden have written about this.

> Dreaming occurs continually, both during sleep and during waking life. Just as the stars persist even when their light is obscured by the light of the sun, so, too, dreaming is a continuous function of the mind that continues during waking life even though obscured from consciousness by the glare of waking life.

To this poetic description we can add a system that allows categorisation. We have night dreams and day dreams. Daydreams can be subdivided into four groups. Daydreams A are fantasies and mind wandering we control. Daydreams B are fantasies and mind wandering we don't control but are conscious of. Daydreams C are fantasies and mind wandering we are not conscious of directly but have a sense of their presence. Daydreams D are fantasies and mind wandering that are unconscious.

*

In this chapter, I have taken you into that 'place' or 'space' before rational thought takes place. The heavy thought of care, to my mind, requires a familiarity and acceptance of lightness, necessitates a journey into the world, shall I say, universe, of dreams. In this universe, we find ourselves constantly wandering within the gravitational force of the unknown.

It is worth hearing the words of Albert Einstein who, as mentioned above, dreamed he was careering down a steep mountainside so fast the stars changed in appearance and on waking formulated his theory of relativity.

> The words or the language, as they are written or spoken, do not seem to play any role in my mechanism of thought. The physical entities which seem to serve as elements of thought are certain signs and more or less clear images which can be 'voluntarily' reproduced and combined... The above-mentioned elements are, in my case, of visual and some muscular type. Conventional words or other signs have to be sought for laboriously only in a second stage, when the mentioned associative play is sufficiently established and can be reproduced at will.

Dream's End

Sleeping to the beat of the night-owl's wing,
Walking through a dream in a dim-lit place,
If a new day dawns the light will sing.

If ascending darkness leaves its sting,
The heart awash, the mind arace,
We won't hear the beat of the night-owl's wing.

Seeds' cradles are their graves. No spring
Swaps winter's depths for grace.
No new day dawns with lights that sing.

But dreams as maps of minds bring
To eyes shapes that hearts erase,
To ears soft beats of the night-owl's wing.

Dream music strums on silent string,
Dream's art paints translucent face,
New days may dawn and lights may sing.

Frightened, faithful, brimming
Eyes find paths through unbound space,
Trusting the beat of the night-owl's wing.
Inhaling dawns with lights that sing.

14

Summoned by the Tides – Emily Dickinson

The Vedic tradition had male and female figures in its pantheon of gods, but those who made contributions within the Brahmodya ritual would have been (predominantly or) exclusively male. Female voices were contained within a prohibited silence. But one female voice has spoken and established its credentials among those who reach for the divine. It outspoke many that have gone before; it extended far beyond the reach of silence.

The voice came from a young woman. In the nineteenth century, she read an article in a literary publication that encouraged aspiring writers. She sent five of her poems to the editor. And a letter which said,

> Are you too deeply occupied to say if my verse is alive?
>
> The mind is so near itself it cannot see distinctly, and I have none to ask.
>
> Should you think it breathed, and had you leisure to tell me, I should feel quick gratitude.
>
> If I make a mistake, that you dared to tell me would give me sincere honour toward you.
>
> I enclose my name, asking you, if you please, sir, to tell me what is true.
>
> That you will not betray me it is needless to ask, since honour is its own pawn.

It was April 1862. The place, Massachusetts, USA. The literary magazine was *The Atlantic*, the editor was Thomas Higginson. The letter was unsigned, a name on a separate small piece of paper – Emily Dickinson.

*

Some years ago, in a Sydney second-hand bookshop, a book caught my eye. It had a shiny green, hardback cover and looked out of place among the tattered paperbacks. Published in 1909, *Famous Prefaces* was a collection of prefaces and prologues of famous books. The contributors included Nicolaus Copernicus, Isaac Newton, Samuel Johnson and Walt Whitman. The introductory note to *Famous Prefaces* said that in a preface, the personality of the author reveals itself and 'speaks with his reader as man to man, disclosing his hopes and fears, seeking sympathy for his difficulties, offering defence of defiance, according to his temper, against the criticisms he anticipates'.

Emily Dickinson never published a book of poetry and therefore no preface was ever written but I would suggest that her letter to Higginson (together with a second written ten days later) be thought of as a preface. In the years before and the quarter of a century following her approach to Higginson, Emily Dickinson wrote 1,778 poems and is now regarded her as one of the greatest poets in the English language. And probably the greatest female poet.

When Higginson replied, he suggested she 'tidy' her poetry. Should we tidy her letter? Who and what do we listen to? To a woman, who although she had a group of friends with whom she shared her poems, was making a huge step into a new world. Her mind, she says, is so near itself it cannot see distinctly. It is as if her poetry is like a living presence inside her. Emily Dickinson was born the year William Hazlitt died. I don't know if she knew of him in 1862 or ever got to know of him, but her sentiments in this letter echo his when he said poetry 'is not a branch of authorship: it is the stuff of which our life is made. The rest is mere oblivion, a dead letter: for all that is worth remembering in life is the poetry of it.'

In his reply, Higginson asked her about family, friends and her education. This is her second letter.

> Thank you for the surgery; it was not so painful as I supposed. I bring you others, as you ask, though they might not differ. While my thought is undressed, I can make the distinction; but when I put them in the gown, they look alike and numb.

You asked how old I was? I made no verse, but one or two, until this winter, sir.

You inquire my books. For poets, I have Keats, and Mr and Mrs Browning. For prose, Mr Ruskin, Sir Thomas Browne, and the Revelations. I went to school, but in your manner of the phrase had no education. When a little girl, I had a friend who taught me immortality; but ventured too near, himself, he never returned.

You ask of my companions. Hills, sir, and the sundown, and a dog large as myself, that my father bought me. They are better than beings because they know, but do not tell; and the noise of the pool at noon excels my piano.

I have a brother and sister; my mother does not care for thought; and father, too busy with his briefs to notice what we do. He buys me many books, but begs be not to read them, because he fears they joggle my mind. They are religious except me, and address an eclipse, every morning, whom they call their 'Father'.

But I fear my story fatigues you. I would like to learn. Could you tell me how to grow, or is it unconveyed, like melody or witchcraft?

Two editors of journals came to my father's house this winter, and asked me for my mind, and when I asked them 'why' they said I was penurious, and they would use it for the world.

I could not weigh myself, myself. My size felt small to me.

This second letter has the same directness that was evident in the first. Her personalty reveals itself. Her thought, she tells, us come undressed, 'but when I put them in the gown they look alike and numb'. Such language presages what awaits us as we read on. 'When a little girl, I had a friend who taught me immortality; but ventured too near, himself, he never returned', a sentence which lets us know she will attend to the sacred subjects, like immortality, but one that is pregnant with mystery and intrigue. Who is this friend who is so important to her? What happened to him in his ventures? Animals, like her dog, 'are better than beings because they know, but do not tell'. We need perhaps to be her 'dog companion' if we are to tune in to the essence of her poems, to listen to her unique voice. We have to allow our mind to be joggled. If we wish our mind to grow, are we ready to be touched by melody? And witchcraft? 'I could not weigh myself, myself' is one of those intoxicating assemblages of words which, if we repeat it to ourselves many times, we will be tuning our ear to what we are about to listen to.

A temptation to tidy her is understandable. Our brain can be inclined to fit her in with other poetic styles. But her unusual features – not giving titles to her poems and using frequent dashes instead of punctuation – is not a sign of eccentricity. I need to listen to her like I listen to no other. Sometimes she hurts the brain. She presents the unexpected right in front of my eyes, in one line, and while I look at it, I become aware there is something going on behind me that beckons for attention.

*

She played the piano, and in her letter said, 'the noise of the pool at noon excels my piano'. Had she been granted a voice at a Brahmodya gathering might she have said,

> He fumbles at your soul
> As players at the keys
> Before they drop full music on.
> He stuns you by degrees,
> Prepares your brittle nature
> For the ethereal blow
> By fainter hammers further heard,
> Then nearer, then so slow
> Your breath has time to straighten,
> Your brain to bubble cool,
> Deals one imperial thunderbolt
> That scalps your naked soul.
>
> When winds take forests in their paws
> The universe is still.

*

The literary critic Harold Bloom said the power of her mind was baffling:

> Except for Shakespeare, Dickinson manifests more cognitive originality than any Western poet since Dante... Though I read and teach her constantly, I remain a bewildered idolater, struggling to understand her enigmatic sublimities.

Only eight of her poems were published in her lifetime and those without her name.

I too am a bewildered idolater and continually try to engage with her enigmatic sublimities. Already, she has taught me many things that assist in cultivating a mind in mindless worlds. The more of her I read and listen to, the more of a novice I feel. I sense that this woman who, as we know, had lived her life in a small town called Amherst, in the country of Hampshire, in the US state of Massachusetts, had a mind so much her own. Just as for John McGahern, the universal was the local with the walls removed. 'Emily Dickinson's poems find in the happenings of village life all that is required to reveal the cosmos,' according to the *Norton Anthology of Modern Poetry*.

She had a vast comprehension of the world. In her garden, in her house, in her poetry writing room, she visited the universe. If we engage with such a person, walk beside her, sit with her as she writes, we get access to the mind of someone who travels to the edge of the human universe. Join her as she reads each newly created poem. Read aloud. Tune in to her unique voice, into her untidiness, the elliptical orbits she will carry you into. Allow yourself to break free from the gravitational pull of common language and be propelled beyond the circumference of your familiar world.

Her way of using words, her untidy punctuation, leave me requiring a way in. Here, Picasso is of help. Some of his pictures seem to take a number of perspectives, looking at the same object or person from three of four positions at the same time. What's it like trying to combine them on the flat canvas? Picasso seemed to use lines that represented each body or object and found a way to achieve his aim. I have no idea if he thought things through in that way but, for me, to think as I have described helps me to explore his paintings of that style.

Now take one of Emily Dickinson's poems.

> The brain is wider than the sky
> For, put them side by side,
> The one the other will include
> With ease, and you beside.
> The brain is deeper than the sea,
> For, hold them, blue to blue,
> The one the other will absorb,
> As sponges, buckets do.
> The brain is just the weight of God,
> For, lift them, pound for pound,
> And they will differ, if they do,
> As syllable from sound.

Thoughts, and words and concepts and images intersect. Throughout this book, I have regularly put the same question: how do we cultivate a mind in mindless worlds? I explore Emily's mind with the same intent with which I have explored the minds of everyone else addressed so far. It's as if I ask them all the same question: how can you help us to care for our minds?

It is in this spirit that I proceed with Emily, and, as always, I have no interest in parsing her mind or any other with the gimlet eye. My sentiments are 'I would like to learn. Can you tell me how to grow? That you dared to tell me… I should feel quick gratitude' – to borrow her words.

One way I learn from her is to study how she treats her own mind. Her poems cover a vast area, from attention to a moment, to a vast expanse of time. They are serious and playful. They are simple. They are profound. We know she read Keats's poems. I'm not sure if she knew his letters, where he described his notion of negative capability. That quality, avoiding an irritable search after fact and reason, infused Emily's mind.

What comes across strongly in her work is respect for the mind. She takes care of her own mind. But she also is aware of the mind's need to time to take in new ideas. She would have made a very good teacher.

> Tell all the truth but tell it slant –
> Success in Circuit lies
> Too bright for our infirm Delight
> The Truth's superb surprise
> As Lightning to the Children eased
> With explanation kind
> The Truth must dazzle gradually
> Or every man be blind –

Just as Hazlitt was a good psychologist, so also was Emily. She was aware of the demons within; tuned in to listen to her unconscious, the fears that can haunt the mind.

> One need not be a chamber to be haunted,
> One need not be a house;
> The brain has corridors surpassing
> Material place.
> Far safer, of a midnight meeting
> External ghost,
> Than an interior confronting
> That whiter host. Far safer through an Abbey gallop,
> The stones a chase,
> Than, moonless, one's own self encounter
> In lonesome place.
> Ourself, behind ourself concealed,
> Should startle most;
> Assassin, hid in our apartment,
> Be horror's least.
> The prudent carries a revolver,
> He bolts the door,
> O'erlooking a superior spectre
> More near.

*

Although Emily approached Higginson as a novice poet, she retained an independence of spirit and continued to write untidily. It was said of Ella Sharpe that she was confident of her virtue in embodying the essentials of psychoanalysis while at the same time being anonymous, meaning she could speak her truth without trying to become famous. Emily knew fame to be a fickle food, so she may have been wary of what it might have done to her. Earlier, I gave Emily a place at the Brahmodya. The Brahmodya is a place where all the sacred subjects leave their names behind. The art critic Christopher Allen:

> Naming is a process that simplifies the world and draws phenomena into systems of human meaning. But whenever we truly pay attention to anything in nature or in human life, we realise how much more complex reality is than these convenient labels suggest; and that is part of what art seeks to reveal to us: the irreducible being of things that lies beneath their names.

Emily unnames herself.

> I'm nobody! Who are you?
> Are you nobody, too?
> Then there's a pair of us –
> Don't tell! They'd banish us, you know.
> How dreary – to be – somebody!
> How public – like a frog
> To tell your name the livelong day
> To an admiring bog!

By unnaming herself, she acquired a freedom that permitted her to unname all the sacred subjects. She had, we saw in her second letter to Higginson, 'a friend who taught me immortality; but ventured too near, himself, he never returned', probably referring to a young man who when she was twenty, encouraged her to write poetry. He died very young. She ventured to the circumference of God, Heaven, Hell, Death,

Soul, Eternity, Immortality, Paradise, Prayer, Bliss, Angels, Calvary, and came back with a poetry that like Shakespeare's takes us to the edge of the mind's reach. Through her simplicity, her intellectual and aesthetic sensitivities shine.

> ONE BLESSING had I, than the rest
> So larger to my eyes
> That I stopped gauging, satisfied,
> For this enchanted size.
> It was the limit of my dream,
> The focus of my prayer,
> A perfect, paralyzing bliss
> Contented as despair.
> I knew no more of want or cold,
> Phantasms both become,
> For this new value in the soul,
> Supremest earthly sum.
> The heaven below the heaven above
> Obscured with ruddier hue
> Life's latitude leant over-full;
> The judgment perished, too.
> Why joys so scantily disburse,
> Why Paradise defer,
> Why floods are served to us in bowls,
> I speculate no more.

She knows when we establish a new point of view, our liberation can in time become a restriction. Her art takes her to the outer limits, to the circumference. She spends time becoming familiar with her new-found space. On the edge of that space, new questions arise and she is off again, thinking and writing herself into the unknown.

Part Three

15

Introduction

Parts one and two mainly focused on how damage can be inflicted on the mind, and general resources that are available for recovery. Part three leans towards renewal. If 'Dublin' is a symbolic place, we can now ask, where do I need to be? How do I want to use my mind? As I go about ordinary business, how do I take care of this mind of mine? And if it surprises me and comes up with the unexpected, will I see it, or pass it by?

What must be respected and underlined is that the world needs our care. We care for our individual mind so we can better serve. Should this be forgotten and the aim become self-aggrandisement, we have fallen into the narrowness of vanity and egotism.

And to continue with the same principles that underpin this book, we are part of a collective, a community of others. One of the greatest moments in human evolution must have been when a bunch of individuals became a collective, when someone risked their own life to save someone else from danger, when we learned that to survive and prosper, we do better, are better, when we work together.

Earlier, in chapters 4 to 8, I systematically examined the issue of clerical sexual abuse of children. This was done from many points of view: historical, political, religious, spiritual, legal, psychological. My argument was that if we neglect or exclude information and knowledge gained from these perspectives, our understanding will be limited. If there is an expectation now that the various strands in this book will be gathered and neatly tied, I will disappoint. Assemble I shall endeavour to do, but such neatness is beyond my intent. The book began in a deliberately conversational style in the hope it would be read as such. If it has opened up a space in your mind, it will have had some success. But I have done my best to advance, keeping in mind what I said in chapter one about Chekhov: 'When a writer takes a pen into his or her hand, they accuse themselves of unanswerable egotism and all they can do with decency after that is to bow.'

Between August and December 2019, I organised ten meetings under the auspices of the Sydney Institute for Psychoanalysis, with the same title as this book. The meetings were billed as lectures and a significant amount of the content of the fourteen chapters you have read was presented. But lectures of the type I have given throughout my life, they were not. I read prepared material, I spoke directly to people, questions and conversations ensued. There was also time for silence. Not those awkward, anxious silences when no one asks a question, but periods when we were all content to wait, the type of waiting a poet engages in when the wrong words or phrases have got onto the page, and the right ones are taking their time.

Of course, as a reader of a text, we are removed from the advantages that a community of people enjoy. We have the written not the spoken word, the page not the person. But all is not lost, because, while there is a lack in one respect, there is a gain in another. My method, as it has been described, set out to incorporate a sense of solitude within the company of others. A silence can be common while at the same time respect the privacy of each and every one present.

The reader is granted the same information and knowledge as is available to the listener. What is enlarged for him or her – the reader, that is – is the space that aloneness offers, a space that is unique to itself.

The reader can tailor to their own reading the ideas offered. They become the mistress of their own thoughts and, as they engage in an internal dialogue between the different parts of themselves, the mind works productivity upon itself.

You can rest assured that the writer, I, have the spirits of Jean

Malaquais and John McGahern at my side. 'The only time I know the truth is when it reveals itself at the point of my pen.' 'I write because I need to write. I write to see. Through words I see.' And the response to Chekhov's warning is to work hard on the art and craft of writing. Malaquais wrote twelve to fourteen hours a day to produce 250 to 300 useable words. McGahern, as I said, took a decade to write his last novel.

Whatever is the way we progress, in community or within ourselves, interpersonally or intra-psychically, there is a forward movement towards the world, towards its care. Each of the remaining chapters are half-written; they are yours to complete. You will make further acquaintance of some people you have already met.

Then there are the new: a man who made a new discovery and kept it all to himself. A man who maintained his identity by years of solitary, secret study, of Time. People who used scientifically constructed instruments to explore new places and people who entered the same spaces guided by the power of imagination.

'Space', 'place', 'earth', 'ground'. As soon as you tie them down, they break loose. And you give up? Or follow?

Do you mind your manners? You soon will, or be invited to.

*

Under the banner of a call to action, I would suggest a week when we all refrain from using terms of demarcation such as baby boomers, millennials, Gen X, Y or Z. It might help us to realise we are all in this together, and when a sixteen-year-old girl speaks eloquently about the dangers of climate change, she is afforded full respect. We who are old have our part to play and, while we still have our faculties, continue to combat the challenges outlined in the opening paragraph of this book.

And here I call up another poet who, until the end, had a determination to remain part of life and of the future. A body may be frail but a mind retains strength when it can produce lines like this.

> And this grey spirit yearning in desire
> To follow knowledge like a sinking star,
> Beyond the utmost bound of human thought.

Alfred Lord Tennyson's mind, not unlike Emily Dickinson's, is always extending itself. It does so to catch up with new demands. It does so to predict; to be prepared. Tennyson's words come from his poem 'Ulysses', and with the ancient story of the *Odyssey* and the notion of a voyage as references points, he speaks of a journey that the mind must take.

He describes the 'waters and a ship',

> There lies the port; the vessel puffs her sail:
> There gloom the dark, broad seas. My mariners,
> Souls that have toiled, and wrought, and thought with me –

I am in no doubt that the work of the mind is to the forefront of his concern.

When I say these remaining chapters are half written and yours to complete, I mean you, young or old, need to step on board. We are all in this world together. If our ship, the planet, goes down, we all go down. Let me return to the lectures at the Sydney Institute for Psychoanalysis. There was a new feature about the series. You could attend in person or electronically, and 90% choose the latter. It allowed people from all over Australia and beyond to take part. I had never 'lectured' in that mode before. It was a challenge to overcome the imaginative adherence we make to the familiar, but as we had an excellent technician on hand to facilitate smooth transmission of sound and image and resolve glitches, we all managed the adaptation to a new and exciting way of communicating.

When the series ended, people wrote to me describing spaces opening up in their minds. One said she was taken aback and surprised at the thoughts she had on a familiar subject. She had never expected her mind to be capable of coming up with an unexpected line of thought.

My own best summary of the experience is described by borrowing

Tennyson's words. Those who took part were my fellow mariners, souls that have toiled, and wrought, and thought with me.

> The night begins to twinkle from the rocks
> The long day wanes: the slow moon climbs: the deep
> Moans round with many voices. Come, my friends,
> 'Tis not too late to seek a newer world.
> Push off, and sitting well in order smite
> The sounding furrows; for my purpose holds
> To sail beyond the sunset, and the baths
> Of all the western stars, until I die.
> It may be that the gulfs will wash us down;
> It may be we shall touch the Happy Isles,
> And see the great Achilles, whom we knew.
> Though much is taken, much abides; and though
> We are not now that strength which in old days
> Moved earth and heaven: that which we are, we are,
> One equal temper of heroic hearts,
> Made weak by time and fate, but strong in will
> To strive, to seek, to find, and not to yield.

*

I carry on aware of what Proust said about the relationship between writer and reader.

> What makes a book and a friend so different…has nothing to do with the greater or less degree of wisdom, but with the manner of our communication, reading, as opposed to conversation, consisting, for each of us, in receiving another's thought, while all the time, ourselves, remaining alone, that is to say, continuing to enjoy the intellectual power that comes in solitude, and which conversation at once destroys – continuing in a state of mind which allows us to be inspired, to let the mind work fruitfully upon itself.

16

Too Bright a Light Blinds

'It is a matter of listening to the rustle of God's cloak and seizing the hem as he passed across the stage of history.' – Bismarck

I write to dead people. It started six years ago when news reached me that someone who I had never met but was important in my life had died. On 30 August 2014, Seamus Heaney was felled. The week after his death, I wrote a poem called 'Engrafting New'. I borrowed heavily to write the poem. The title was borrowed from Shakespeare's sonnet 15 which ends with 'And all in war with Time for love of you/As he takes from you, I engraft you new.' I engrafted lines from three of Heaney's poems. Those lines appear in italics.

Knowing three other pieces of information will help make sense of the poem. Firstly, the word *ceis* appears in the poem. *Ceis* is a Gaelic word. It means a small wicker bridge. Secondly, John McGahern (who was a friend of Heaney) died in 2006. Thirdly, in rural Ireland when a person died, neighbours called to the house to express condolences. When the grieving family have had enough callers, a sign went up on the door or the gate which said, 'House Private'.

Engrafting New

So far I've avoided the obituaries,
The great eulogies. Later perhaps.
For now, mourning is quiet; house private.
I have him all to myself.

His passing was a great blow.
Sure we were only getting used to
McGahern going when this fellow
Heaney ups and leaves, for good.

Is there anyone else to turn to?
Hold on! It is as he'd foretold it'd be:
Big soft buffetings come at the car sideways
Catch the heart off guard…blow it open.

A spring dawn enters the room.
His poems enter my heart,
Crisp as a silvered frost,
Fresh as a first reading.

And when I speak them loudly,
His deep-planted words flow leisurely.
There's a new step in my voice.
I'm hearing things I've never heard.

The light that is his shadow shines,
Shows new paths, ceises, crossings,
Stepping stones, stairways to
Richer, deeper, greener, inner lands.

The space he has vacated is for us,
Luminous emptiness.
A warp and waver of light.
Sunlit absence.

The heft and hush of him is now
A bright nowhere,
A soul ramifying and forever
Silent, beyond silence listened for.

You might say, of course, that this way of writing is just one step from impersonating a dead person, as I did in chapter 3 with Sigmund Freud.

With Heaney, I needed silence to mourn. The world had lost him, but I did not want the thoughts, and words, from that world to get in the way. If you have lived a life knowing about the summons of the tides, in which you have learned you have to wade through griefs to become someone, there is hope in achieving light at the end of the mourning tunnel.

A refusal to pass over personal grief when others urge you to move on is captured in Shakespeare's *Macbeth*. Having killed the king, Macbeth decides to get rid of anyone who stands in his way. Banquo is the first to be murdered. Then Macduff and his family are to be slaughtered. In Act IV scene iii, while Malcolm and Macduff consider the state of the country, Ross enters with news that Macduff's wife and children are dead.

In what is one of the most painful depictions of loss and grief in literature, Malcolm cries out,

> Merciful heaven!
> What, man! Ne'er pull your hat upon your brows;
> Give sorrow words. The grief that does not speak
> Whispers the o'er-fraught heart, and bids it break.

Macduff asks questions of Ross as Malcolm calls for immediate action and revenge and sees it as a cure for grief. Macduff ignores Malcolm. He counts out in words the fullness of the loss that Ross has reported.

> All my pretty ones?
> Did you say all? O hell-kite! All?
> What, all my pretty chickens and their dam
> At one fell swoop?

Again Malcolm promotes revenge and says he should

> Dispute it like a man.

But Macduff will not be rushed. He will not be pushed into reactive mode. Malcolm can't see it, but Macduff has put up a sign that reads, 'House Private'. He lets Malcolm know that in his own good time he will dispute the wrong like a man.

> I shall do so;
> But I must also feel it like a man.
> I cannot but remember such things were,
> That were most precious to me.

For me, a few years passed. With August in the air, something from the intervening years called out. What came onto the page that time was a step towards what I could call a letter-poem.

Before offering it, if his body of work is not easily accessible, a few details may situate the sentiments.

The notion of crossings figured in Heaney's work. Stepping over a bridge, a stream, a path, could represent simple acts of necessity or a movement from one stage of life to another, or even from life to whatever may or may not be beyond.

During the troubles in Northern Ireland, Heaney's cousin was murdered and in a poem, his shade returns to enlighten and to speak. Heaney also wrote a number of poems about bodies discovered in the peat fields of Jutland. Then we have poems about everyday physical activities like using a shovel to move gravel, a spade to dig potatoes or a bricklayer wielding a trowel.

When my 'House Private' sign came down, the many obituaries and eulogies were there to be read, as were letters to rhe editor in newspapers all over the world. Of all of them, the briefest was the most telling. It was in *The Irish Times*. I did not know the man but saw from his address he lived close to where I was born. His letter: 'Sir, I am saddened. As a nation we are a man down.'

I wrote this.

Hymn for Heaney

The weeks and months were moving past
And now the years are flowing too,
Birch, beech and alder leaves are falling fast,
We lift our eyes and turn our thoughts to you.

You laid down stepping stones for our comings
And our goings, sang hymns in praise of bogs
And sunsets, coal men and eel fishermen.
You led the long dead back to light, granted passage

Their epitaphs to write. Dig down, dig deep
Spread roots within well anchored words and
Like masted trees be firm to bend in stormy times.
You said all this, or words to this effect.

You taught us as you were taught – that mind is vast.
And you like Dante's Virgil our trusty guide, our how-to
Man, trowel-lifter, spade-wielder. Your poems your life outlast
Our hearts renew; fresh shoots our minds imbue.

*

Being in contact with the dead is important for thinking. Fear, taboo, the idea that religions have a freehold to that ground, may cause us to pull back should we see a glimmer of light coming from that direction. The adjectives pile up: old-fashioned, morbid, dour. But this ground is precious and needs to be fought for. Dangers exist when you step on it. Proust pointed to one: you can become overawed and then silenced in the magisterial presence of great books and works of art. But that obstacle is easily overcome. Those who bow down and are stifled by the greatness of people past are already (if you watch them closely) idolatrous towards the living. Some figure in the world today commands their allegiance. And they have within themselves an internalised authority figure, domineering, requiring submission.

If we have removed obstacles, may we proceed and, as Auden reminded us, take part in 'breaking bread with the great dead'.

*

My other correspondence with the departed is a different story. A letter came to me. Well, not quite. She wrote it to the world. I extensively read her poems and listened to recordings of them, so it wasn't a huge leap to conjecture that she wrote to me. I didn't know if anyone had replied to her but, as 150 years had elapsed, I deemed it polite to attempt a reply.

We know there are many factors external and internal which resulted in only a handful of Emily Dickinson's poems being published in her lifetime. Internally, there was a reticence in her expressed in her words, 'Fame is a fickle food/upon a shifting sand.' But I believe in her self-belief, her conviction that one day her work would be highly valued. After all, one of her great inspirations, Shakespeare, was content for the personal details of the life behind the creator to drift away into time.

Maybe she would appreciate, even enjoy a – very much delayed – reply.

To introduce my letter-poem, I will, as with Seamus Heaney, provide a context and note some of her poems I allude to in mine.

Firstly, her poem.

> This is my letter to the world,
> That never wrote to me,
> The simple news that Nature told,
> With tender majesty.
>
> Her message is committed
> To hands I cannot see;
> For love of her, sweet countrymen,
> Judge tenderly of me!

Receiving a letter was always a treasure for her. She would take it to the quiet of her room and, to use her words, 'Then draw my little letter forth / And slowly pick the lock.'

When people came to visit, she sometimes gave them flowers. At times, she was unable to come from her room. One reason suggested for this was her fear of having an epileptic seizure. Her mind travelled to the flowers fading in the friend's vase and she wondered if she had remained in their heart.

> I hide myself within my flower
> That fading from your vase,
> You, unsuspecting, feel for me
> Almost a loneliness.

The making of a poem could be for her, 'The spreading wide my narrow hands / To gather Paradise.'

And the poem was of fragile substance, like gossamer on twigs, a flimsy structure holding delicate life. 'How frugal is the chariot / That bears the human soul.'

I wrote this to her.

> Your letter to the world arrived,
> 'Twas subject of much talk,
> We opened wide our hands
> And hearts - to unpick its lock.

> We had a sturdy barge
> For evening's passing toll,
> But you said – it is frugal poems
> That best bear the human soul.

> Poems should be – alive, you said,
> Undresssed – or else be numb;
> And swift must be the mind
> And the spirit lithesome.

Sacred subjects lightly touched,
God in nature – seen,
The known unnamed – reveals
The essence of a being.

You looked to north, east, south
And west and – to nowhere
And caught a glimpse of light sublime
An answer to your prayer.

In faintest scent of hidden flower,
The silver sparkle of the dew,
We found the magic in your words
And judge tenderly – of you.

17

The Mind as Navigator

'To my mind, no one lets humanity down so much as those people who study knowledge as if it were some sort of technical skill.' – Seneca

During his three great voyages, Captain James Cook discovered the islands of the Pacific. On returning to England, he brought objects and people from these places. He was hailed as the greatest explorer and discoverer.

But the people who lived in these places did not think of themselves as 'discovered'. Their islands, their seas, were their homes. Their stories linked them to the places their ancestors inhabited for centuries. Maori arrived in what is called New Zealand 1,000 years ago. The land mass we call Australia, 'discovered' a few centuries ago, had been inhabited for 60,000 years.

Cook and the Europeans who followed brought the Western scientific mind to Australia. Nothing like it had shaped the people, their lives and their land. They did not know mathematics and physics. Methods of experimentation that emerged in the Enlightenment were beyond them. They had no system to record words. Their minds were mystical. The stories they lived inside. They, their lives and their stories were interwoven and at one with their country. Instead of written records, their knowledge lived in the spoken word, celebrated in ritual and passed down by word of mouth. Notions of subject and object, of stepping outside an experience and viewing it from a distant stance, were foreign.

The Western scientific mind Cook and the Europeans brought had its own painful history. It had casualties, like Bruno. But its success in changing the world was considerable. And the practical benefits it brought to ordinary life were enjoyed by millions. People lived longer, healthier. They were relieved of much suffering. But most of all it changed people's minds. This Western mind had an interesting formation. The art critic Christopher Allen wrote about this. He said,

> Modern science arguably arises from the confluence of two traditions. One is the heritage of classical Greece, which gave us the confidence that human reason could understand nature; but the other is the Judeo-Christian tradition, which places reason ultimately outside nature. For the medieval mind, the world made sense only from the perspective of God, who stood outside creation. Humans could achieve a degree of understanding of the universe by striving to conceive it from God's point of view...although our minds are not capable of assimilating the divine vision, even if we are permitted a momentary glimpse of the ultimate truth of the universe.

The Renaissance reclaimed the Greeks' confidence in the human mind, and that is why its interest in the theory of perspective is so much more than a device for pictorial composition. It was a metaphor for the intelligibility of the world from the point of view of the human mind. Yet the nascent also inherited the sense of seeing nature from the outside, from a privileged vantage point beyond the living world itself. It was this combination that determined the specific quality, and ultimately the power, of this new kind of knowledge. The new science was predicated on a clear distinction between the knowing subject and the world of objects; and that objective world of matter, as Descartes later defined it, is quintessentially defined by extension, or quantifiability. Everything in the objective would can be defined by size, shape, mass, location and so on, and scientific laws describe the regularities in the behaviour of objects under different circumstances.

When Europeans arrived in Australia to a land fully, if scarcely by their standards, populated – with hundreds of nations and hundreds of languages – they decided it was a *terra nullius*. Convenient, you might say, to justify a land grab. But what was behind that? Were they incapable of comprehending the Aboriginal mind? Did their 'science' see ignorance? Did their 'enlightenment' see primitiveness? Maybe they had lost contact with their own history, that in the not too distant past their own ancestors lived this way.

Einstein wondered what was in the empty space between the visible objects, planets, stars, asteroids, et cetera in the universe. Gravity, he said to himself. And the electromagnetic field. But something drove him on. And on he went, and realised the electromagnetic field is not inside empty space. The electromagnetic field is that space.

*

When Europeans began to sail through the Pacific Ocean, they had their charts and scientific instruments and recorded readings and weather events in ledgers and logbooks. Polynesians had neither writing or instruments and it was presumed their presence on the islands in such a huge expanse of sea occurred by chance, drifting with the winds and currents.

But while they had no physical maps, the whole network of islands and the distance between them and the navigational routes to travel from one to another, were imprinted in their minds. Without chronometers and sextants, the whole world, the world they knew as whole, was mapped in the collective mind, assembled over generations, transmitted orally and in many cases committed to song.

They observed the sun by day and the moon by night. They took account of the winds, the waves and sea currents. The flight paths of seabirds, the behaviour of dolphins and porpoises were all watched and entered in their mental store of knowledge.

A navigator sat in a special chair at the front of the light wooden, fast-moving craft. He and all of the guild of navigators were highly esteemed. They were a part of a group that comprised the living and the dead. All accumulated knowledge was a living entity. Their survival depended upon it. No single navigator in his lifetime would visit all of the more than one hundred islands in the network but he knew the whole on the map of his mind.

On a single journey, the navigator was not allowed to sleep, day or night. Before departing, he visualised the journey ahead and, until they reached their destination, he continued to look at that image. And while he looked at it, he read the changing conditions and the course was set on his advice.

*

Reverting to a position of disbelief in the navigational skills of Polynesians in the nineteenth century is understandable if we allow for the minds of many being mesmerised by new scientific advances. But it is an intersection that is worth pausing at. In human history, maps, charts and instruments are relatively recent aids to the traveller. Wayfinding is as old as the hills and what the Polynesians did on water took place on land ever since humans, and their animal ancestors before them, set off to journey beyond the horizon.

The Inuit, who, it is said, have a hundred words for snow, developed their method of navigation. Australian Aboriginals read the land and the sky. Holding the place you set out from in mind, remembering routes, skymarks and landmarks, mapping spaces within memory and developing a means to transmit information to others were all essential to survival and progress. Like the Polynesians, Aboriginal Australians, through songlines and Dreamtime stories, created maps in the mind that were passed down through generations.

*

Science can degrade into scientism. The *OED* defines scientism as, 'excessive belief in the power of scientific knowledge and techniques, or in the applicability of the methods of physical science to other fields, especially human behaviour and the social sciences'. Captain Cook with his own eyes saw the navigational skills of the Polynesians and believed they could travel without scientific instruments.

At periods throughout the nineteenth century, when there was great excitement as one new scientific discovery followed another, the belief in their navigational skills waned. When this scepticism resurged, old myths re-emerged. One was the theory that the Pacific islands were the peaks of drowned continents. The 'natives' of all the islands were stranded there. It was impossible that they could have navigated from one to the other.

A more recent example of scientism can be found if we look at the history of what is called 'evidence-based medicine', EBM. One strand in this story in the UK takes us to newly qualified doctors, who when they worked with older doctors who were wedded to out-of-date practices, argued that treatment should be based on the newest evidence. Their highlighting of this issue led to many beneficial changes and new codes of practice. However, along the way, in some quarters, scientism took a hold and this led to some of the original architects of the change saying it had gone too far.

This book has argued for pluralism. No single point of view, no single method of exploration and investigation leads to knowledge of human beings. It may tell us a lot about the brain but little about the mind. We can't have a God's-eye view of the world. There is no view from nowhere. Science is one way of thinking. As soon as you ask, how do you measure the thing that allows you to measure things, you have to look elsewhere. When we try to marry our subjective experience of ourselves with an objective, scientific explanation, tensions and possibly divorce threatens. Someone has made a good attempt at describing the dilemma. You can walk around a city and in various places find maps for tourists with a red dot marking where you stand at that moment. As you move about, you see another part of the map and the same red dot. However, at the tourist information centre, the map of the city that you receive will have no red dot. Science may be our best way of mapping the external world, but it has its limitations.

*

Cartography

How did I come here? How did I find a way?
Those clean and finely-contoured maps
I followed in the morning, faded under midday suns.

Much of what and where and who I visited
Was unexpected. That man I saw ahead not he
Who I've become. Midway, I made my dreams my barge

And found myself on shores of inner worlds,
With silence, science and poems my guides.
Making marks upon time's sands, (like Birnam Wood)

The impenetrable wilderness has come to me.
The beauty of images is found in front of things;
The beauty of ideas, behind. Moon replaces sun.

18

Old Ground

'I longed for the night as the poet might do, the true poet who feels himself inhabited by a thing obscure but powerful, and who strives to erect images like ramparts round that thing in order to capture it. To capture it in a snare of images.' – Joshua Reynolds

> He had no more need of days and weeks and months,
> The particular year was of no account, and when asked
> To name the prime minister of Australia he declined.
> Mind you, these days that changed so often, if found
> Not to know he would be forgiven and excused.
>
> He stepped back from all these minor matters and retreated;
> Not so much a retreat as a return. He had no need
> For walls and doors; no love of the high-rise.
> His was open ground (where anyone could come and go)
> Ground that had since time immemorial been walked
>
> Upon and watched over, tended and sown by poets.
> Here once the spoken word had reigned supreme,
> The music and the sight of sound repeated from
> Generation to generation. Here words were first
> Chiselled into rock. Here parchment and berry ink

Came into vogue. Manuscripts and books arrived,
And the printing presses, and then the internet.
He didn't care. They were all the same to him,
All means to an end. Surrounded by riches
Every morning he just sat and waited while

Seeds scattered by the world's poems germinated,
Sprouted, made flowers and leaves and branches
And full-grown trees. And when the sun danced
Upon his face or the moon silvered his already
Silver hair, or the wind blew louder and longer

Than had been foretold, or darkness removed all
Curves and lines and demarcations, it mattered
Not at all. And if he spoke little it was not he had
Nothing to say. He was past the waste of time.
He just waited. There was so much listening to do.

19

Where Silence Reigns

'Oh, how often one longs to speak a few degrees more deeply! My prose…lies deeper…but one gets only a minimal layer further down; one's left with a mere intimation of the kind of speech that may be possible there where silence reigns.' – Maria Rainer Rilke

I had to hear *ghaoth* out loud to provoke my aural memory and imagination. Was it that my unconscious mind wanted more that explains the following? Fifty years ago, as a schoolboy, I first read and learned large sections of Alfred Tennyson's poem 'Morte D'Arthur'. Then, for decades I forgot about it, until one day, browsing in a second-hand bookshop, I found an old anthology of English poetry. When I read the first line, the words and the music of the poem flooded back. I could close my eyes and reliably recite pages.

In the poem, King Arthur tells of how he received his sword Excalibur from the maiden in the lake.

> In those old days, one summer noon, an arm
> Rose up from out the bosom of the lake,
> Clothed in white samite, mystic, wonderful,
> Holding the sword – and how I row'd across
> And took it, and have worn it, like a king.

Poetry is no respecter of time, or place. That is one of its great strengths. In the summer of 2008, I was in Lane Cove Park in Sydney looking down on the river. It was evening. The scene came alive. I wrote,

It hasn't rained for weeks.
From such stillness wonders are born
from water such as this

Tennyson's magic maiden's arm
'clothed in white samite, mystic, wonderful,'
rose with King Arthur's sword Excalibur.

The jewels of your nightfall, the poetry of your dreams
mystic moments of your past, will rise and shine and reach
beyond your half-forgotten days.

The Irish poet Rupert Strong said that the poet picks up a bow and sends an arrow back through the centuries. My experience in the bookshop was of an arrow coming forward from the centuries from the nineteenth to the twenty-first.

Stillness is one of the most precious qualities in life. In today's world, where frenzied communication is god, it is a rare commodity. Patrick and Brigit were told by their church that God was found in the stillness of prayer. But their priestly abusers destroyed that stillness. An after-effect of trauma is the absence of stillness and it is the impossibility of silence inside the mind of the traumatised that is most damaging.

Many voices in this book say that poetry was for them an internal life force. Hazlitt named it as that fine particle within us that lifts our whole being. Edward Dyer encouraged us to treat our minds, and the space within us where self-consciousness resides, as a kingdom.

When you can live with silence and stillness, your words find a hidden key, and everything you hear and speak changes. Stillness isn't a static place where nothing happens. Silence makes room for imagination, inspiration and the capacity to listen.

This book uses short and long poems. Length does not matter. Each attempts to capture an atmosphere. All the poems, my own or those of others, draw on the poet's personal experience. But the personal only has relevance if it wanders into the experience of others, dovetails with another life and draws strength from it. Therefore, a poem's success rests entirely on whether it can be called a piece of art. A poem is a piece of art if it allows you to take it into yourself. We can return to Joyce stating that a piano is a coffin of notes that requires a pianist to play it. And to McGahern that a book is a coffin of words requiring a reader to bring it to life.

Stillness is a condition that promotes privacy. Privacy is another precious commodity that in today's world is under rapacious assault. (A metaphor of biblical allusion is appropriate here. Privacy is a pearl of great price that is often traded as worthless.) Fiction – poetry, short stories and the novel – are great defenders of privacy. If the writer has done his work and created that piece of art, he should glide into the shadows and leave the reader free, in the privacy of his own mind, to imagine things that are exclusively his. Good fiction writers are never instructive. They are present, but at an intimately respectful distance. The artist, according to Flaubert, should not appear any more in his work than God in nature: present everywhere, but nowhere visible.

The artist needs to retain a certain childlike innocence, a natural trust that his inner nature will guide him. 'An artist,' we heard from Charles Morgan, 'is a child who stares…not at the flower or the drop of water or the face.' The child/artist looks not at the imprisoning walls of life, but outward through a window where the opaque becomes the serene.

Visitation from outside, from beyond, is a frequent theme in spiritual traditions. We might speculate as to the nature of the visitation, but there would be general agreement on two counts: it is mysterious and it is outside the power of the visited. Here, traditions overlap and to some a poem or any piece of art that is a response to a visitation, can be considered a prayer, a prayer to the universe, or, as Teilhard de Chardin would suggest, a hymn to the universe.

Having a sense of the poetic is like a sixth sense. But that seems an inadequate description. I would be happier with a description that addressed the expansion of our already existing senses, and the way those senses interact and assist each other. Poems try to capture moments of sensual transition, periods – often brief and ephemeral – where one sense gives way to another, where two (or more) senses overlap or where they each refract different aspects of the same reality.

The poet is not some special creature existing in a rarefied sphere. He is part of the blood, sweat, tears and joy of life. Rilke described the place of the poet in his essay 'Concerning the Poet'. Sixteen oarsmen row a boat upstream. The currents are strong; the task demanding. They pull as one, with outstretched arms, rising from their seats, meeting the forces of nature with determination and respect. A passenger, a man seemingly of no consequence, sings a wordless song. His voice rises and falls. Everyone listening lift their eyes and look into the distance beyond.

When Louise Glück gave her acceptance speech on receiving the 2020 Nobel Prize, she talked of the poets who had influenced the way she wrote and what she wrote about.

> I was drawn 'to the solitary human voice, raised in lament or longing. And the poets I returned to as I grew older were the poets in whose work I played, as the elected listener, a crucial role. Intimate, seductive, often furtive or clandestine. Not stadium poets. Not poets talking to themselves. I liked this pact, I liked the sense that what the poem spoke was essential and also private, the message received by the priest or the analyst.

*

I returned to my diagonals. Here is a completed poem written six decades later after the first diagonal travelled across the paper.

The Gift of Writing

It began with a lead pencil
And a crooked line
The teacher called diagonal.
It ended with a book, his name
Upon the dust cover.

He was taught to strive for
Sentences that rode the thermals,
Words that called like bugles
Or whispered softly in the ear.
Or in your steps stopped you still.

Someone said a pen can be
An artist's brush; you can paint,
Lay down shades of colour
Beyond the black and white.
So, as he did strive the child

Inside, tongue between teeth,
Hope riding high gripped
The pencil, pushed, prayed,
Implored the line –
Be straighter than the last.

20

Here is Where I Start From

'Nothing is at last sacred but the integrity of your own mind. Absolve you to yourself, and you shall have the suffrage of the world.'
– Ralph Waldo Emerson

If you grow up by the sea, the smell of the sea gets into your bones. In the valleys, you breathe the valleys. The seafarer and the hillwalker can come to know each other, but each will carry within what shaped them. We all are influenced, have ways of looking, means to make sense. I've moved countries and continents, literally and figuratively. I enjoyed travelling to the places I have spent time in in this book, but as I see the end, I should acknowledge the place from which I have done much viewing. It is a particular, some might say peculiar, position. It is where I have spent many years of my working life.

Back in chapter 3, you heard me (speaking as Freud) inviting you to try something out.

> This step you must take if you are to fully understand what I am talking about: you need to lie on the couch. Use that most wonderful of human faculties, your imagination. Lie back. Allow yourself to enter into that in-between world.

Everyone who ends up sitting in an analytic chair starts there. In that position, free to say whatever comes to mind, in the presence of another, you learn to know yourself. Then, when other people come with their suffering and you suggest they lie on your couch, you don't forget their courage, cognisant of the fact that you were once in the same position.

There is a basic belief that runs through and connects this whole book and without it my whole edifice would crumble. It is an acceptance of an unconscious, and a recognition of its place in everyday life. Most people acknowledge some form of unconscious, or preconscious. Reminded of something forgotten, it is described as drifting away and now returning. At a minimum, their unconscious is like a basement, an attic, or conceived as a storage facility where what is presently unwanted and unneeded is stored.

The unconscious I perceive goes far beyond such a function. Opening a window into any dream experience is one entry point into what is a dynamic, alive, vibrant part of the mind. I shudder to think what mankind would be without it. We would not be 'human'. There would be no creativity, no imagination, no art, no outrageous inventiveness. And, God forbid, no poetry.

Describing her psychoanalysis, Louise Glück said,

> [In my analysis] I was learning to use native detachment to make contact with myself, which is the point, I suppose, of dream analysis: what's utilised are objective images. I cultivated a capacity to study images and patterns of speech, to see, as objectively as possible, what ideas they embodied. Insofar as I was, obviously, the source of those dreams, those images, I could infer these ideas were mine, the embodied conflicts mine. The longer I withheld conclusion, the more I saw.

Most of all, the unconscious is untidy. And should we hope to tidy and tame it, we will be on the same path as those who seek perfection and sainthood with all its accompanying dangers. Tidying the unconscious would be as misleading and as futile as tidying Emily Dickinson's poems.

The smallness of a place can belie the size of what you can see from there. A man may travel the earth but never leave his village. Every place visited becomes to him a reflection, for better or worse, of what his home looked like. A man may not travel far, but in his mind, he has seen the world.

'The local is the universal with the walls removed,' John McGahern said. A passage from *That They May Face The Rising Sun* illustrates this. Jamesie, who seldom left the area he was born in, says to Ruttledge, the traveller, 'I may not have travelled far but I know the whole world.' 'You do know the whole world,' Ruttledge said. 'And you have been my sweet guide.'

Ella Sharpe told us that despite the limited confines of her life as an analyst, she experienced a rich variety of living that became part of her, that never would have been hers either to experience or to understand, but for her work.

> I contacted all sorts and kinds of living, all imaginable circumstances, human tragedy and human comedy, humour and dourness, the pathos of the defeated, the incredible endurances and victories that some souls achieve over human fate.

*

Our quest will always bear the marks of our life and times and set out from the conditions in which we find ourselves in our world. But as/if we travel back through history, through the great cultures we will find many instances when people put their minds to the care of thinking.

The Fool in *King Lear* is one of the play's hardest-working characters. He and Lear have known each other all their lives, but Lear is losing his mind, regressing to a blind narcissism, destroying the public order by dividing the kingdom. While any knowledge he acquired is slipping through his fingers, the Fool tries everything he can, from humour to damning criticism, to direct confrontation to guide Lear back to regaining his mind. The tragedy of Lear's life, in the Fool's estimation, is his failure to acquire wisdom. 'Thou shouldst not,' he tells Lear, 'have become old before thou hadst become wise.'

From wherever we come in place and whenever in time we live, are we not all trying to find our way to our own 'Dublin'? Not a place on any map in any country. Rather a space within.

In chapter 12, 'To Infinity, And Beyond', I occupied a piece of ground. As I stood there, I could look around, at the present world and worlds past. Various people came to dislodge me. My occupying the place was to them illegitimate. Some tried persuasion, others threatened.

The notion of 'place' has stretched like a thread through this book, the island in *The Tempest*, Richard Dyer's kingdom, William Hazlitt's country. As the book developed, the thread of place divided and while location remained relevant, a new strand emerged, the notion of 'space'. Much of part two opened up spaces. The shift from place, defined with emphasis on the concrete, to space defined with emphasis on the symbolic, was a huge evolutionary development for mankind. Our species became Homo Sapiens when it occurred.

*

A Compass Line of Light

A rudder holds a compass line of light.
A silver vessel silent on a silver sea.
An absent breeze the patient sails invite.

On distant shores two staring eyes alight,
Unknown, unnamed. It may be you. Or me
If the rudder holds our compass line of light.

Traversing far off lands can consume a life,
Always on the go, intrepid travellers we
Fear the absent breeze. Our impatient sails invite

Any forward thrust. Stillness is a plight.
Scanning flickering stars, we but faintly see
Our inner rudder's compass line of light.

A silver sea inside holds no fear of night.
Storms subside. The heart expectant, free,
No absent breeze desires. The patient sails invite

Time to heal, time to write, art to delight.
In poetry's vessel all faults pardoned be;
In tempest, its rudder our compass line of light,
Its breath the breeze our inner sails invite.

21

Building Blocks

'I am straining at particles of light in the midst of a great darkness.'
– John Keats

Building Blocks is a see-saw piece. That's how I describe a piece of writing, within a large project, that you address and say, you're in, you're out, you're in, you're out! Or I say to myself, you've said that already, or that is so basic there's no need to mention it.

A few things convinced me to let it make the final cut. I put it in for myself because I need to keep what it says in mind. Secondly, if a concert violinist takes the time to play scales, to keep in touch with basics, shouldn't we be reminded of the basic building blocks of thought? My mind was finally made up while watching an eminent public figure I much admired, interviewed by two young journalists. He barely addressed the questions of one and completely ignored those of the other, behaving as if she didn't exist.

Don't do that, I told him in my mind.

So, here is that voice again, talking to myself, talking to you.

Things to do. Things to not do.

A few answers. Many questions.

*

When a new item enters my field of observation, where do I begin? Do I trust my senses? Or is my intellect permanently in the starting blocks? Is it safe to vegetate, to give myself over to the experience I am presented with?

How do I listen to new information? Am I observant about its source? Is the messenger honest? Does he feel reliable? Has he taken time to gather facts? Is he a reactor or a responder?

Presented with an incomplete image of a familiar subject, our brain fills in the absences and we 'see' the whole. However, if our mind operates in an equivalent fashion when presented with incomplete information, we run the risk of reaching a false conclusion. Alternatively, we regard the filled-in part as provisional or probable and postpone judgement.

What state of mind am I in at this point? Am I in reactive or response mode? Am I inclined to say something just for the sake of saying something? Within my mind, is there a space or place where I can entertain a totally new fact and keep it there long enough to assess its true value? Or its uselessness? How closely and carefully can I listen? If I start to listen well, can I maintain that wellness? And as I engage in observation, information gathering and listening, have I put aside a percentage of my mind to oversee the workings of my heart and mind?

Do I have a calm and objective referee inside me, who even in a grand final, when the score is tight and the stands filled with passionate intensity, maintain fairness for all?

*

It is often at the listening stage that things go wrong. If proper attentiveness is in place, later rulings are easier to call. Listen to this. A red traffic light means stop. It's green to go. That's what the rule book says. Yes?

Do you answer yes? If so, yes to what? You stop on red. OK. Do you go on green if a person steps in your path? You'd stop! So, to answer yes is inadequate. And the adequate answer is go, provided the path is clear. But we're still not done. I asked an extra question with the words, That's what the rule book says. Yes? When I was a learner driver, the Irish rule book it put it that way. Red means stop. Green means go, provided the path is clear. My enquiry had compressed two questions into one.

A belief can creep in that there is such a thing as a perfectly working mind. Nonsense. And if we try too hard to have one, we stumble. We can't eradicate our personal, idiosyncratic tendencies and leanings. Like a stringed musical instrument, the perfect pitch will not hold indefinitely and we go out of tune.

Sometimes, the voices that are raised against political correctness are trying to draw attention to such impossible expectations. Hazlitt rightly warned against this. Each of us is a bundle of all sorts of things. What is crucial is that we know the particular bundle we are and keep that percentage of ourselves doing the job of the good referee.

The dangers of seeking perfection are very real with significant consequences. I've always had an unease with the notion of religious or secular sainthood. While we should not doubt the extraordinary achievements of some, where halos are allocated, the risks outweigh the possible benefits. Objects and places of association become relics and goals for pilgrimage. Such deification is misleading. Mostly this beatification or canonisation waits until death. In some cases, it is in motion while a person is still alive. On his deathbed, St Francis of Assisi's person was being fought over by two groups claiming ownership of where and what was important to him, so they could establish the location they lived in as the true site, thereby reaping all the spiritual and temporal advantages of exclusivity.

A second instance returns me to an earlier observation concerning the origins of sharia law within the Islamic tradition. There, the Prophet's daily routines that he used to support a meaningful and mindful life were described. Being a practical man, he understood the need for order and procedures, to act as guides and support and give structure to a busy day. It is a waste of time to start every day unstructured, to wake up to a complete blank and plan anew every morning.

Later on, when the spirit that inspired his life seemed to have been lost sight of and laxity was deemed to have set in, what was done? We know what was done. Legislation drafted and practice codified. It would be hard to tell if the original intent was simply to offer guidance (history shows us how easily the new powers rewrite the record), but we do know of the degradation that occurred, and soon (and presently) severe punishment, including capital punishment, beheading, stoning, enforce compliance.

Belief and myths of an original ideal place (Eden), or time (Golden Age), may have arisen from a human need for innocence as a beginning, and as a hoped-for end. In my scheme, they are important reference points in the long and arduous labour of learning to think. A mind without a capacity to conceive perfection is like a square without sides. The Canadian write James Slater suggested that

> It is only in books that one finds perfection, only in books that it cannot be spoiled. Art, in a sense, is life brought to a standstill, rescued from time. The secret of making it is simple; discard everything that is good enough.

*

And what of laughter? That most extraordinary invention. A man once said to me he did not believe in God, but he knew that if he ever came to such a belief, laughter would have played a large part because only some almighty genius could have invented it.

I speculate. The birds were here fifty million years before us. When our ancestors, the chimpanzees, chattered in the treetops, did one of them, one day, tire of chattering? There was silence. A bird sang. A million years passed. The chimp, his brain a little altered listened longer, shook his head and instead of reaching for another piece of fruit or branch to chew, found the sound of his chatter changed. The rudiments of something akin to a thought came to him. The wonder of the birdsong contrasted with the monotony of his own voice. A smile lit up his face. And he laughed. At himself.

I shouldn't wager much on whether my speculative fiction is based on any semblance of reality. But given the fact that one of the most beneficial usages of laughter is when we can laugh at ourselves and that a sense of humour is a reliable sign of emotional and mental health, I'm happy to place a few bob each way.

*

If these blocks are in situ, the issue of criticism can be placed upon them. The whole nature of what criticism is, is changed by having foundations such as these. Criticism becomes a shared search for truth as distinct from what is false. It's not a competition. It's a collaborative enterprise. And soon we are free to reach for and use the word judgement. Being 'judgemental' falls away. It has no place here. If a place is claimed for it, it signals that one or more of the building blocks have moved or been knocked out of place.

When shared understanding is arrived at, shared judgements may be made. With the situation clarified, the problems identified we move to what needs to be said, what action is required to bring about a change. Thought is greater than having something in your mind. Mind is greater than calling yourself mindful.

And if, inside myself, I sense a seismic movement, a hunch that my building blocks might be moving out of place, to steady myself, I call back to memory those words that Hazlitt wrote about Joseph Fawcett. No flaw in the clear mirror of his mind. Open to impressions; strenuously engaging them. What he wanted was something to make him think. He enriched the soil of his mind with continued accessions of borrowed strength and beauty. That delicious feeling – to like what is excellent, no matter whose it is.

22

Listening and Learning

'A man should learn to detect that gleam of light which flashes across his mind from within, more than the lustre of the firmament of bards and sages.' – Ralph Waldo Emerson

Some years ago, I ran a workshop in Sydney. It was called Creativity: How to Listen and Learn. It could be described as an effort to combine the Western mind and the Aboriginal mind. Indeed, the concept of the workshop was shaped by many of the ideas and people you have already read about in this book. I also make the point that understanding needs embodiment. Good ideas should be put into practice. I provide a detailed description of the workshop. This is how I advertised the event.

This workshop explores ways of listening to one's own creativity. Most humanly creative moments arrive unannounced; they are outside the control of our rational minds and are the product of our imagination and come from our unconscious. Nowadays we have instant access to the libraries of the world and are bombarded daily with information from all parts of the globe. In our educational systems, too much time is dedicated to accumulating information and following other people's minds, and too little time is spent listening to what we hear internally.

We meet once a week for four weeks. Each meeting lasts 80 minutes. At the first meeting I will speak for 40 minutes. It will not be an academic paper and the presentation will draw mainly on literature. During the second 40 minutes all members are free to speak but are asked to refrain from asking for clarification or elaboration from the speaker. The general ethos governing this part is similar to the process of a Quaker meeting: anyone so moved may speak; they speak to express themselves; they speak to the whole meeting; silence is an acceptable response.

In the time immediately after the meeting and in the week until the next meeting all participants are asked not to enter into conversation with anyone, either inside or outside the group about the meeting. My reasoning for this is that we often inadvertently give away good ideas before they have time to germinate in our own mind.

To enable everyone to hold on to such thoughts and to listen for them there is some 'homework'. You are asked to do two things: firstly, to keep a diary to allow a conversation with yourself about any thoughts you have about the experience, and secondly to write free-associatively for at least ten minutes between each meeting. Free-associative writing involves writing whatever comes to your mind no matter what it is. It is best done without stopping and thinking. Just let the pen or keyboard have a life of its own. Do not worry about grammar, punctuation, order or sense. Once written, do not re-read it. Turn the page or close the document. You can do more than ten minutes in the week if you wish.

In the time between the first and second meeting I will devote a number of hours to assembling some thoughts for the second meeting and will present a second paper which will also last 40 minutes. I will use my experience of the second part of the first meeting as my starting point. I will not summarise the responses of the participants or order them into any coherent form.

When we assemble a week later for the second meeting you are asked not to bring your diary or your free-associative writing. Instead you are encouraged to listen to the presentation. Again, there will be forty minutes for talking.

This pattern will be repeated twice: in other words, there will be three presentations and three periods to talk.

The fourth and final meeting will be a review and evaluation of the process we have been involved in. In the days before the final meeting all participants are asked to read their diaries and their free-associative writing.

One reason I refer back to this event is that it underlined how we can often inadvertently give away good ideas before they have time to germinate in our own mind. In that seminar I created a context to draw attention to that process and to find ways to prevent it happening. What passes through our mind, given that we are social animals, can immediately seek out another person to communicate with. I think it important to slow down that process. It is of course central to responding, as distinct from reacting. It is essential also to cultivate our mind as a creative space.

23

Good Manners of the Mind

'Ah, but a man's reach should exceed his grasp/Or what's a heaven for?' – Robert Browning

Nowadays, to initiate a conversation about manners is likely to raise eyebrows. That – the raising of eyebrows, I mean – would in the past, with those who saw manners as all important, been frowned upon. OK. I accept, it is hard not to poke fun, not least because it is not long ago that good manners were instilled in every child. Books were written on the subject and even schools set up for the same purpose. Obey your elders, they know best! Elbows off the table! We have all suffered in the observance; and hopefully delighted in the flouting.

However, if we get serious and pull the debate back from the absurd and the ridiculous, the most cynical among us would have to acknowledge that good manners have a place in social life. Few could hold the line where rudeness to everyone, all of the time, without consequences, is tolerable and fewer still defend a claim that the way we treat others and want to be treated ourselves is unimportant.

When we place the debate in the middle of ordinary life, we see that good manners go beyond artificial practices. They have a moral dimension. They speak to respect, to ways of listening to others, to a regard for privacy.

There is a form of address in Gaelic that has always had a poetic resonance for me, not quite holding the power of *ghaoth*, but nonetheless significant. When taught to write a letter in Gaelic, in place of 'Dear Mr', you wrote, *A Dhuine Uasail*. The manner of address probably had its origins in the lost Gaelic aristocracy. It means literally, 'noble person'. An 'h' softens the letter before it, the 'd' is almost a 'g'. It is pronounced, *A GUINE-ou-sell*.

However, I am not here launching an extended conversation about good manners as modes of action and behaviour. Instead, I am opening a door into a conversation about what can be referred to as good manners of the mind. In the space that is the privacy of our mind, do we consider good manners to be important and relevant? Perhaps I am saying to you, come inside the mind and let's pose the question, are there such things as good manners of the mind?

Take an instance of Newton or Galileo. Here, the pursuit of knowledge was described as an exploration of the mind of God. If you described your pursuit in a different way, how would you respond? This is not an archaic question. Nowadays, there are many competing world views. When they meet, does respect frame the encounter? Is *A Dhuine Uasail* an apt address?

William Hazlitt's foundational thinking about disinterestedness created the conditions for good manners of the mind, that ability to move into the mind of another and show respect. Despite having fierce disagreement with a political thinker like Edmund Burke and finding his traditionalism abhorrent, he nonetheless could see that Burke had given time and thought to assembling his building blocks. Burke distinguished himself from bigots whose only retort was a reactive one.

Hazlitt's friend Joseph Fawcett had good manners of the mind. 'He gave a cordial welcome to all sorts, provided they were the best in their kind. [He likes] what is excellent, no matter whose it is.' He was not fond of counterfeits or duplicates because they did not respect good manners of the mind. As the opposite of egotism, Fawcett felt gratitude for the contributions of other minds. People like him, Hazlitt said,

> acquire by habit a greater aptitude in appreciating what they owe to others. Their taste is not made a sacrifice to their egotism and vanity, and they enrich the soil of their minds with continual accessions of borrowed strength and beauty.

In 1988, John McGahern's fifth novel, *Amongst Women*, was shortlisted for the Booker Prize. The central character in the novel is a man called Moran, who was once an IRA fighter, and his past deeds are described in the story. When McGahern attended the presentation dinner at London's Guildhall (he didn't win), he was upbraided by the critic A.N. Wilson, who accused him of glorifying violence and the IRA. It was clear to McGahern during the altercation that Wilson hadn't read the book, and his attack was itself an act of mindless violence, the very thing he claimed to decry.

McGahern's good manners of the mind were in evidence in his refusal to react. Instead, he responded, and at a later date, in writing.

> *Amongst Women* glorifies nothing but life, and fairly humble life. All its violence is internalised within a family, is not public or political; but is not, therefore, a lesser evil. If the novel suggests anything, it is how difficult it is for people, especially women who until recently had no real power in society, to try and create a space to live and love in the shadow of violence.

In out-of-the-way places, humans dig deep into the earth searching for precious gems. Hidden within some deeply buried literary texts gems can be found. In the 27 October 1906 edition of the *British Medical Journal* there is a gem called 'The Growth of Truth', written by William Osler MD. Nine days earlier, he gave the Harveian oration at the Royal College of Physicians in London. He used his speech not only to acknowledge Harvey's work on the circulation of the blood, but to talk about the growth of truth. In doing so, he displayed great manners of the mind.

He declared his

> deep respect for the mighty minds of old and a keen appreciation of the importance of the study of history. The lesson of the day is the lesson of our lives. History is simply the biography of the mind of man. And our interest in history, and its educational value is directly proportionate to the completeness of our study of the individuals through whom this mind has been manifest.

For me, an outstanding gem in Osler's talk is the statement that in science, today's startling innovation can become tomorrow's burden. Humans become attached to their discovered truths and

> sooner or later, insensibly, unconsciously, the iron yoke of conformity, is upon our neck, and in our minds, as in our hearts, the force of habit becomes irresistible.

Good manners of the mind protect against this. They do so by presenting a truth and then detaching the mind from that truth, never grasping it too tightly, always creating space for further growth, for another mind, that in time might add or subtract.

Good manners in a mind leave space all around it. Others may fill it. Or into that space the first mind may expand. Either way, there will be a celebration, a cordial welcome, because the best of its kind has arrived. Thus, the soil of many minds is enriched with borrowed strength and beauty.

If good manners of the mind are born out of a respect for, and a dependency upon, others, they reflect the natural order of things. Great minds, great in the sense of being original, depend on lesser minds. The inventor, the true creator, can be so taken up with their construction that they are unable to communicate to others. Preoccupied with the essence of their creation, they can't make links with what already exists productively in the minds of others. Their invention, like a flying machine, hovers, unable to land. Possessive of good manners of the mind, they defer to other minds to, as it were, prepare a safe landing site. And they experience gratitude to those who take the time and put the effort in, to mark continual lines where they have provided a broken pathway pointing to riches.

*

Charles Darwin concluded *The Origins of Species* with the following paragraph:

Thus, from the war of nature, from famine and death, the most exalted object of which we are capable of conceiving, namely, the production of the higher animals, directly follows. There is grandeur in this view of life, with its several powers, having been originally breathed into a few forms or into one; and that, whilst this planet has gone cycling on according to the fixed law of gravity, from so simple a beginning endless forms most beautiful and most wonderful have been, and are being, evolved.

Good manners of the mind are more likely to be safeguarded if we seek and admire not only truth but beauty. Beauty is a powerful force, in nature, in art, in life. Beauty is a powerful force in thought. There is beauty in knowing. We speak about intellectual beauty.

Beauty is in the eye of the beholder, it is said, but I say, there is beauty in the mind of the beholder. The beauty of the human face and form, of art, of nature is beheld when we perceive it. The beauty in and of the mind is apprehended by the mind.

Shakespeare wrote numerous sonnets about beauty in its many forms. Some might say he anticipated the age of the selfie. In Sonnet 69, he described those who may look upon the beauty of the human face, admire and praise, but also look further and 'look into the beauty of thy mind'.

Following strands of beauty and truth may be fraught. Walk through a maze of magnets in a metal suit. Knowledge is so frequently grabbed, exchanged for cash, traded in the service of egotism and vanity. It's a triumph to get through the maze.

Like Shakespeare, Emily Dickinson explored beauty in her own enigmatic fashion.

> Beauty be not caused, it is
> Chase it, and it ceases,
> Chase it not, and it abides.
> Overtake the creases
> In the meadow, when the wind
> Runs his fingers thro' it,

Deity will see to it
That you never do it.

Freeholders of a piece of land, a farmer or a horticulturist, only borrow it. Their rights are not everlasting. They will die and someone else will take over. To try to overtake the creases in the meadow when the wind runs its finger through it is futile. Beauty that we try to possess will simply slip through our human fingers. Behind what we can know is our attitude to what we know. Claiming a freehold on the beauty of knowledge is doomed. Deity, powers greater than yours, will see to it that you never do it.

In 1865, Matthew Arnold, the Victorian critic and poet, praised the Irish writer Edmund Burke for his capacity to take up a position that opposed his own. Burke wrote about the French Revolution, and argued strenuously against it, but concluded his piece by admitting that the opposite point of view might have some validity. Arnold wrote,

> That return of Burke upon himself has always seemed to me one of the finest things in English literature, or indeed in any literature. That is what I call living by ideas: when one side of a question has long had your earnest support, when all your feelings are engaged, when you hear all round you no language but your own, when your party talks this language like a steam-engine and can imagine no other, – still to be able to think, still to be irresistibly carried, if so it be, by the current of thought to the opposite side of the question... I know of nothing more striking.

Burke was interested in beauty. If the opposite side of the question was not just interested in truth but also displayed beauty, he acknowledged and admired it.

Good manners of the mind are fostered by truth. We can never claim it as a freehold possession, but we can work to live each day in its proximity. Beauty, like truth, some say, is worth living and dying for. Beauty is truth, truth beauty, is all we can know or need to know, according to John Keats.

In exploring the motivation of the scientist and why someone would spend a life labouring to understand, Henri Poincaré acknowledged the part played by the wish to advance and improve the lot of humanity. But beyond such reasons, he pointed to another, an overarching driving force, namely, a love of beauty.

> The scientist does not study nature because it is useful to do so. He studies it because he takes pleasure in it, and he takes pleasure in it because it is beautiful. If nature were not beautiful it would not be worth knowing, and life would not be worth living.

What I Do

Some rush headlong. Some stand and wait. Some kneel
And reach under the surface of the great reservoir,
And slowly, moved first by instinct, then by music
And by mind, lift up their hands, liquid full, overflowing.

Practising my art, my craft, that is what I do.
Then I pour a liquid mirror and offer it to you. I trust
My thoughts and words, your heart and mind, align.
I hope my hands will rise with water turned to wine.

24

Feathers on the Breath of God

'At 73 I learnt a little about the real structure of nature...when I am 80 I shall have made more progress; at 90 I shall penetrate the mystery of things...when I am 110, everything I do, be it a dot or a line, will be alive.' – Katsushika Hokusai

In 1930, Sigmund Freud was awarded the Goethe Prize for Literature, an award given for one's talents as a writer. In 1915, he, along with other writers, was invited by the Berlin Goethe Society to write an essay for a commemorative volume called *Goethe's Country*. It was a good cause; the money from sales went to support libraries. The essay Freud wrote was called 'On Transience'.

> Not long ago I went on a summer walk through a smiling countryside in the company of a taciturn friend and of a young but already famous poet. The poet admired the beauty of the scene around us but felt no joy in it. He was disturbed by the thought that all this beauty was fated for extinction, that it would vanish when winter came, like all human beauty and all the beauty and splendour that men have created or may create. All that he would otherwise have loved and admired seemed to him shorn of its worth by the transience which was its doom.
>
> The proneness to decay of all that is beautiful and perfect can, as we know, give rise to two different impulses in the mind. The one leads to the aching despondency felt by the young poet, while the other leads to rebellion against the fact asserted. No, it is impossible that all this loveliness of Nature and Art, of the world of our sensations and of the world outside, will really fade away into

nothing. But this demand for immortality is a product of our wishes too unmistakable to lay claim to reality: what is painful may none the less be true. I could not see my way to dispute the transience of all things, nor could I insist upon an exception in favour of what is beautiful and perfect. But I did dispute the pessimistic poet's view that the transience of what is beautiful involves any loss in its worth.

On the contrary, an increase! Transience value is a scarcity value in time. Limitation in the possibility of an enjoyment raises the value of the enjoyment. It was incomprehensible, I declared, that the thought of the transience of beauty should interfere with our joy in it. As regards the beauty of nature, each time it is destroyed by winter it comes again next year, so that in relation to the length of our lives it can in fact be regarded as eternal. The beauty of the human form and face vanish for ever in the course of our lives, but their evanescence only lends them a fresh charm. A flower that blossoms only for a single night does not seem to us on that account less lovely. Nor can I understand any better why the beauty and perfection of a work of art or of an intellectual achievement should lose its worth because of its temporal limitation. A time may indeed come when the pictures and statues which we admire to-day will crumble to dust, or a race of men may follow us who no longer understand the works of our poets and thinkers, or a geological epoch may even arrive when all animate life upon the earth ceases; but since the value of all this beauty and perfection is determined only by its significance for our own emotional lives, it has no need to survive us and is therefore independent of absolute duration.

Freud wrote this essay at the same time as one of his central books, *Mourning and Melancholia*. There, he attended to loss and how necessary it is for the mind to learn to grieve. Ungrieved loss can lead the mind in two directions: we spend every waking moment running away from it, doing everything possible to avoid it; our mind is overcome by it, disabled and dominated by depression.

'On Transience' is written from a place in the mind between those two extremes, the space where living takes place, where precious life can be heard in the music of words, sensed in the lilac blossom, relished through the gift of imagination. 'On Transience', in my reading, is the closest Freud came to writing like a poet.

The important thing for me now, as I edge closer to writing this book's end, is to draw attention to those who know, and have shown us, how to keep our mind in good order, how to be open to the transient, how to recognise and relish those moments when the mystery at the heart of our existence presents itself for our contemplation.

> To be,
> Or never to have been,
> Not how, or Who created
> The simple fact of Being,
> That the animate and inanimate
> Are.

*

'A Feather on the Breath of God' is a phrase handed down through the ages from Hildegard of Bingen (1098–1179). She was an abbess, philosopher, teacher, theologian, medical scientist, physicist, dramatist, painter, poet and composer. She recorded this story about a king sitting on his throne, which was surrounded by huge columns ornamented with ivory. Banners flew bearing the kings name. He picked up a small feather from the ground and placed it in the palm of his hand. He blew on the feather and it floated through the air. 'You and I', he is reported to have said, 'are no more than feathers on the breath of God.'

What are the conditions that create the state of mind where the transient can be apprehended? Marcel Proust described the position he would take up when he left his room and went out to the garden in Combray to read.

> I would go on with it in the garden, under the chestnut tree, in a hooded chair of wicker and canvas in the depths of which I used

to sit and feel that I was hidden from the eyes of anyone who might be coming to call upon my family. And then my thoughts, too, formed a similar sort of recess, in the depths of which I felt I could bury myself and remain invisible even while I looked at what went on outside.

Among the 1.5 million words in *In Search of Lost Time*, Proust gives us many glimpses of his mind at work. When he next tells us about himself as he looked out from his garden chair, it provides a clear window to view his mind as he glimpses the transient.

When I saw an external object, my consciousness that I was seeing it would remain between me and it, surrounding it with a thin spiritual border that prevented me from ever touching its substance directly; for it would somehow evaporate before I could make contact with it, just as an incandescent body that is brought into proximity with something wet never actually touches its moisture, since it is always preceded by a zone of evaporation.

Refrain from too tight a grip; respect the space between what is beautiful and your desire to possess it; let your consciousness keep a separateness, he seems to tell us (therefore encouraging good manners of the mind).

The exquisiteness of Proust's description led me to estimate highly the value of a poem learned by heart, and I decided that when the poem itself is of considerable worth, the investment of our time and labour spent in rote learning is repaid a hundredfold each time we recall it; and moreover reciting it aloud to ourselves lets us hear those musical chords whose roots lie deep in the subsoil of our aural life, enables us to transcend those borders, those translucent veils, those mystical, transient, in-between spaces whose magic he had captured, and so we lose and gain ourselves and are at one with the poem and the poem's creator.

A writer who appreciates the transient, who accepts that he or she is no more than a feather on the breath of God, is an instrument to assist others. To the Polish poet Anna Smir,

A poet becomes…an antenna capturing the voices of the world, a medium expressing his own subconscious and the collective subconscious. For one moment he possesses wealth usually inaccessible to him, and he loses it when that moment is over.

Far Side of Time

See you on the far side of time.
It is not a place.
There are no signposts.
You walk alone.

Trust ancient symbols, sounds
Which pre-and post-date words,
Ambient touch,
Scents that are indescribable,

Visions opalescent,
Crepuscular,
Slender as gossamer,
Offered to the inner eye.

Strands searching for
The spirit of thought,
Must need await,
Their braiding

25

'Hope' is the Thing

'Art is that chalice into which we pour the wine of transcendence.'
– Stanley Kunitz

>'Hope' is the thing with feathers –
>That perches in the soul –
>And sings the tune without the words –
>And never stops – at all –
>
>And sweetest – in the gale – is heard –
>And sore must be the storm –
>That could abash the little bird
>That kept so many warm –
>
>I've heard it in the chillest land –
>And on the strangest sea –
>Yet – never – in extremity,
>It asked a crumb – of me.

Like many of Emily Dickinson's poems, 'Hope is the thing with feathers' allows you to look many ways.

Two stories from Romania illustrate how, in the lives of two men, battles were fought internally and externally, to permit the bird of hope to perch upon the soul. One an actor, the other a philosopher, went to great lengths and did unusual things to maintain a private space in their minds where they were free to think.

Having freed Eastern Europe from Hitler's scourge, Stalin extended his own reign of terror beyond Russia's borders. In Romania under Ceaușescu, Communism took on its own repressive form where scraps of freedom were hard to find. In police states, thinkers and artists are a particular threat. This is not surprising. Artists and philosophers provoke free thought; as creators of art and ideas, they embody the free flow of the imagination.

Marin Moraru was a prominent Romanian Shakespearean actor. After he retired, he gave an interview in which he talked about the rehearsals for a production of *The Tempest* at the National Theatre in Bucharest. He was playing Caliban, and they rehearsed for nearly two years. However, just before the premiere, state censorship considered that production of *The Tempest* inappropriate and cancelled it.

'My Caliban would have been a great Caliban,' said Marin Moraru in that interview, 'because I had discovered something new and extraordinary in Shakespeare's text.'

'What?' the host asked him.

'Something that only I had seen. But I'm not telling you.'

Years later, Moraru was interviewed again and asked what was it he had discovered in Shakespeare's text. Again, he refused to answer.

Pressed and asked, 'Wouldn't you like to share your discovery?' he said no and offered the following explanation to the interviewer.

> I'll tell you something, although you'll probably not get it. When the censorship cancelled our production, I was devastated. I was devastated because I knew I'd never have another chance to play Caliban. "God, what will happen to my Caliban?" I asked myself obsessively, but there was nothing I could do. Then, after a few years, the very thought that I alone in the whole world had seen something new and extraordinary in Shakespeare's *The Tempest* gave me a joy of an intensity I'd never known. That joy has never left me, and today it's as intense as it was when I first felt it. I don't know how to put it. It's been like an inner overcoat; one that nobody can rob me of, as long as nobody knows about it. I don't think I can go on without it. As an actor, I used to think that it's all about being on stage; well, it's not. I see from your face that you don't get

it. How could you, when sharing has become a global ideology? I told you that you'd probably not get it.

The second story is about Alexandru Dragomir. Born in 1916, he studied philosophy and law at the University of Bucharest. He went to the University of Breslau in Poland to learn Greek, Latin and German. Then he enrolled as a doctoral student at the University of Freiburg im Breisgau under the supervision of the philosopher Martin Heidegger. The war interrupted his studies and he left without completing his degree. In Romania, the Communists seized power in 1947. Dragomir's position was dangerous. As an intellectual, he was considered a threat, but his links with Germany further increased the danger.

To preserve his life, he embarked upon a plan to make himself anonymous. If he stood out, he would be identified in a regime that demanded obedience and uniformity. He did a variety of jobs and worked as a welder, a clerk, a vendor, an accountant and economist. Dragomir survived and lived to see the fall of the regime. He was seventy-three in 1989, when Ceaușescu was overthrown and executed.

The life of this well-educated man was spent doing menial jobs or work for which he had no natural inclination, but under the radar he lived another life. He continued his study of philosophical texts in Greek, Latin, French, German and English and when the regime fell, he gave lectures to a small circle of philosophers. When he died in 2002, a hundred notebooks were found among his belongings. They contained ideas he had secretly worked on. However, although he shared the content of some notebooks with the circle, others were kept private. They contained ideas about time which he had worked on for decades. Much research is taking place on these notebooks and parts of them have been published.

But at this stage of the story, I am led back to Moraru, because both men seem to me to have done something similar. What Moraru and Dragomir found was what I found when I made diagonals. This is my page, my square, my pencil, my hand. Underneath the pile of expectations, fear, intimidation and threats, there is an incipient self, an 'I'. The chilliest lands and the strangest seas may strive to extinguish it. Like Moraru and Dragomir, each and every person must nurture and protect it. If the creative ease and determination that held the pencil lightly and firmly live on, a path will always be found.

Dragomir worked with a man who approached him in private one day and said he wanted to tell him something, but he must never tell anyone else. He must have picked up that Dragomir valued privacy, because he told him the name he was known by was not his real name. He was 'Ion' to everyone. To Dragomir he was now 'Napoleon'.

So now we have three! Moraru with his insight into Caliban; Dragomir with his deliberations on Time; Napoleon with his name. All bear witness to an 'I', to a precious sense of privacy, to a part of their own soul that cannot, need not, ever be made public.

How can it be public, when in private we have limited knowledge of its extension? Emily Dickinson often takes us to the borders of the self/soul and sometimes she is beyond us, on the edge, beckoning us to join her in her travels. As Heraclitus said thousands of years ago,

> You could not discover the limits of soul, even if you travelled by every path in order to do so; such is the depth of its meaning.

In chapter 22, Listening and Learning, I described my attempt to open minds to the above. Do we ask what Moraru found in two years of rehearsal to be Caliban? What did he come across and later, through mourning and thought, come to know? Am I tempted to guess? No. I should not. Rather, I should continue to learn from Moraru and value what he has taught me.

Most opportunities of this nature are lost because we reach for the less important thing. We don't acquire as precious a possession as Moraru acquired,

> something new and extraordinary...a joy of an intensity I'd never known...that has never left me, that today it's as intense as it was when I first felt it...I don't think I can go on without it.

Instead of waiting to let something grow within, we borrow from another or we copy someone else.

Moraru was part of a group who for two years, read, spoke, listened, played their parts. 'It's not all about being on stage,' he said. It is about creating a space inside the mind. Others can assist, help with the circumstances. But an act of personal creation is involved.

Shakespeare's poetry in *The Tempest* assisted Moraru in creating a life-giving space within himself. Donald Pendergast's teaching offered his pupils in 1840s Ireland the chance to learn about anything. Poetry is the antithesis of reactivity. It is pure response. Despots and totalitarian regimes rage against it because of the freedom it excites. 'How with this rage shall beauty hold a plea / Whose action is no stronger than a flower?' Shakespeare asked. This freedom is beyond the despot's and the regime's control.

Queuing for meagre rations in a freezing gulag, a woman approached the Russian poet Anna Akhmatova and asked if her poetry was up to the job of describing the conditions they were forced to endure. She said it was.

It is about being somewhere else. It is about becoming someone else. It is about allowing the thing with feathers to perch upon the soul.

To continue its flight into our world today, I wrote a poem, about birds and poets, called 'On Birds and Poets'. The Arctic tern or sea swallow can live for thirty years. On its migratory life it travels 1.5 million miles, the equivalent of three return journeys from Earth to the Moon. Liu Xiaobo was a Chinese poet and Nobel Peace Laureate. He wrote of the bloody crackdown in Tiananmen Square in 1989. He was incarcerated by the Chinese Communist Party. He died on 13 July 2017 and was quickly cremated and buried at sea. Once, when freed from incarceration, Liu Xiaobo was asked how we coped with life in a cell. Fully expecting that the knock on his door could come at any time, he explained that in China there are two types of prisons. One was defined by four walls, the other by the boundaries of the country. Everyone who lives in a state where freedom of thought and of expression are forbidden, lives in a prison.

Of Birds and Poets

A bird who dies in flight falls vertical through cloud,
Small heart that beat a trillion beats grows tired,
Slender strength dissolves, wings falter, cease to glide
Plummets to the ground. A ragdoll cast aside.
But a strange thing happened. (My eyes I fear deceived),
The arms of earth extend, a great wanderer received.
Earth – many trillion tonnes to its bosom holds the tern
Who weighs a hundred grams. As a breeze will sway a fern,
Or rustle leaves on tree tops, as mist bejewels snowdrops,
As sparrow's fall, to this life's end, the call to us – attend.

A poet who dies respected, his words like silver rays
Is cherished and remembered and lights up all our days.
Liu Xiaobo died imprisoned and was cast into the sea,
They hoped he'd be forgotten, unloved, by you and me.
But a strange thing happened. The sea rejected lies
And from his ashes strewn a flock of birds now flies.
There's one in every tree and all corners of the land
Are by a canopy of silver singing spanned.
Liu Xiaobo's life is lost, him we all must mourn,
But as we read his poems his spirit is reborn.

He said the darkness one day will cease,
We'll wake to freedom's songs of peace.

26

Places on Earth

'I think poetry is a vital part of our intelligence, our ability to learn, our ability to remember, the relationship between our bodies and our minds.' – Robert Pinsky

> A clean-skinned, flesh-coloured angophora stretched its limbs.
> On its fingered extremities a lorikeet lands. It sings.
> I don't suppose it has any sense of privilege or knows I envy
> It its call, its technicoloured coat, its vantage point, how it is free
> To swoop; can make a perfect arc. But I can imagine its wings being
> Mine. I rise, I swoop, I arc, I touch the fingertips of the divine.

We are earthly creatures. Our first place on earth is always important to us. If we leave it by choice it comes with us. Should we lose it by circumstance, or have it ripped from us, we will forever know its loss. Its presence or its absence makes heavy or light the steps we take as we move through our life. In ancient Celtic spiritual tradition, the landscape was deemed to evoke a sense of the divine. To leave the place of your birth, the place where your early identity was formed and to which you remained attached, was for some an experience of martyrdom. It some ancient texts, it is described as white martyrdom.

The land I now live on is vastly different from my first place on earth. Instead of birch, beech and alder trees, I look out to angophoras, blue gums and jacarandas. The cockatoo, the currawong, the rainbow lorikeet and king parrot have replaced the robin, the blackbird and the corncrake. But when Aboriginal people talk about land and Country, I feel at home. Their monuments are nature-made. And when they tell stories and feel the presence of their ancestors or read the Dreamtime in a star-studded sky, I am aware that all of us, no matter where we were born or live, are bound in love and gratitude to this same planet. The land draws us inwards, to the ancestors of the self that we are, that we have become through incorporation of the spirits that were there before us, to the community that welcomed our creation and celebrated our life.

If you have travelled this far, I, accepting the counsel John McGahern offered to writers, must bow down to the reader, grateful for the trust and time spent negotiating rickety crossings, exploring space. And may the shortcomings of the book be forgiven and annulled by your creativity and courage. If poetry has extended the nature and quality of your thoughts, I shall be most gratified. But if you have arrived at a clear and distinct definition of poetry, I would be saddened. The essence of poetry is not found in the words on the page resting in their form. It is not found in the heard or spoken words. Neither does it reside in the stamen of the flower ready to be plucked. Even your mind and heart cannot encase its essences. Its essence is the flash of light you have never seen before, in the space you have stepped into for the first time. It is a *ginninderra,* an Australian Aboriginal word (adopted by the publishers of this book, Ginninderra Press) which describes a small flash or ray of light, one that provides direction and gives hope within darkness.

Those who, once upon a time, after staring at the stars, stared at their own minds, saw small flashes of light. Poems are attempts to follow that light. If the light is overcome by darkness, we start again, to seek the true poetry is an invaluable starting point to get us back on the right track. As Patrick Kavanagh exhorted us, 'And you must take yourself in hand / And dig and ditch your authentic land.'

And Louise Glück:

The true has about it an air of mystery or inexplicability... It is essence, ore, wholly unique, and therefore comparable to nothing. No 'it' will have existed before; what will have existed are other instances of like authenticity. The true, in poetry, is felt as insight. It is very rare, but beside it other poems seem merely intelligent comment.

The examined life is worth living because nothing quite like 'it' has ever existed. Your life becomes your yours by the way you live; as mine becomes mine. Each of us has an air of mystery and inexplicability. Is the essence of a life the challenge to authentically communicate that mystery and inexplicability to each other?

On the first pages of this book were mapped some of my earliest footprints, while an appreciation of the beginnings of each and every one of us pervades all its pages. I conclude with 'My Place on Earth', not from nostalgia but from a recognition that all our pasts live on inside us and we extend the freedoms of the present by remembering the past, our gains and our losses our sorrows and our joys.

My Place on Earth

A solid monument a stone wall ten feet high fifty feet long
stands as witness and there is no breath no sign of life
there is peace all is quiet the quiet and the peace that lives
where life has passed and yes the silence stretches into infinity.

A visitor today a newcomer to this place might remark
upon the unremarkable stone wall ten feet high fifty feet long.
It's a boundary wall between a garden and a haggard.

I've been here before fifty years ago this wall was
the back wall of a long line of sheds that housed cattle.

Stand with me where that row of daffodils bloom
along this line another wall stood with wooden rafters shouldering
a red corrugated-iron V-shaped roof that covered three sheds
one for milking cows one for bullocks one for calves.

Come and step over the daffodils past the crocuses
and the budding roses step into the middle shed
into the middle of an Irish winter
walk between the bullocks their steamy breath like mist
rising from a marsh these big brutes spend their time
eating farting shitting butting they'll brush up
against you but no harm will come of that.

It's the middle of summer now and the shed's been empty for weeks
the beasts spend the milder months outdoors
we used to fill a sack full of straw and tie a rope to the rafters
a perfect swing and here in the manger
in that small clump of uneaten hay the Rhode Island Red
would lay her eggs and old Danny Gearon
with waist coat and blue-striped collar-less shirt
stood at the farmhouse door the eggs in his hat
and our mother scolded us and told us
to stop sniggering and staring at Danny's
pasty-white bald-headed eagle head.

Next door where the cows were milked
was a quieter place a loose chain around the beasts' necks
kept them separate and safe
here time passed unnoticed and when I sat on the wooden stool
pail between my knees my head resting against her hip
ready to push if I felt the kick
the sharp rat-a-tat-tat of the milk as it hit the metal base
turned to a soft rhythmic purr as the pail filled
creamy whiteness rising swaying holding my world in balance.

In the top shed many a calf came into the world and hit the
strawed floor with a thud its mother's tongue licking it to
life urging it on and up uncertain legs unwavering
instinct finding the mother's teat drawing the beestings.

Come around to the haggard – or rickyard as it was sometimes called –
the life that went on here was anyone's business
as a boy – I was three or four – I remember the old thrashing mill
the sheaves pitched up and fed down into its belly
dust flew hessian bags filled with golden grain
loose straw spewed out the back
and the chaff-man with stinging eyes and golden beard
a latter-day Hermes demoted in the ranks
caduceus turned pitchfork in hand.

That was July or August but June now June was a much-loved month
the swaying meadows row upon verdant row bowed to the
sun-god whose love and light performed a trans-substantiation
from green to gold-nectared crackle-dry sweet-smelling hay
domes of architectural delight dotted the fields
and the hay bogey like a magic carpet with ropes and rackets
conspired like faith to move mountain after small mountain
and deliver them into the expert sculptural hands of the rick-man.

Inside the wide-eyed trusting stillness of childhood
we neither travel back nor venture forth
time is un-measured because it can't be measured
life is lived in the fragrance of the present
each single silent-movie scene
– dust motes in a shaft of sunlight
– a belching monster mill
– a god of chaff in amber preserved
– a bullock's watchful eye
– soft yellow hoofs on a new-born calf
– three brown eggs in a well-worn hat
– pail brim-full of warm milk
– the sweet sweet smell of new-mown hay
cradles and caresses you in its angel wings
moment by moment by sacred moment.

I can see that life has increased and other lives have flourished
and multiplied since I've been here
and if truth be told this piece of earth and this place
in its present form and manifestations and me
are strangers now people walk this earth
drive tractors and combine harvesters
dig gardens plant daffodils and crocuses and roses
that never knew me to forget me
and the ground where once my
world stood and was all I knew
is to them unknown unknowable and never to be mourned.

Bibliography

Aciman, Andre. (2021) *Homo Irrealis*. Faber.
Armstrong, Karen. (1999) *A History of God*. Vintage.
— (2014) *Fields of Blood*. Penguin.
Arnold, M. (1970) *Selected Prose*. Penguin.
Berlin, I. (1990) *The Crooked Timber of Humanity*. Fontana.
— (1996) *The Sense of Reality*. Pimlico.
Bloom, Harold. (1999) *Shakespeare: The Invention of the Human*. Fourth Estate.
Burke, Edmund. (1998) *A Philosophical Enquiry into the Sublime and Beautiful*. Penguin.
Calasso, Roberto. (2002) *Literature and the Gods*. Vintage.
Dawkins, Richard. (1986) *The Blind Watchmaker*. Penguin.
— (2006) *The God Delusion*. Penguin.
Dentith, S. (1995) *Bakhtinian Thought*. Routledge.
Fairbairn, W.R.D. (1952) *Psychoanalytic Studies of the Personality*. Tavistock.
Fogol, G. (1991) *The Work of Hans Loewald*. Jason Aronson.
Buxton Forman, M. (1960) *The Letters of John Keats*. Oxford University Press.
Freud, S. (1953–73) *The Standard Edition of the Complete Works of Sigmund Freud*, 24 vols. James Strachey (ed.). Hogarth.
— (1900) *The Interpretation of Dreams*. S.E. vol. 4 and 5.
— (1916) *On Transience*. S.E. vol. 14.
Franklin, R. (ed.) (1999) *The Poems of Emily Dickinson*. Harvard Press.
Glück, Louise. (2012) *Poems 1962–2012*. Harper Collins.
— (1994) *Proofs and Theories: Essays on Poetry*. The Ecco Press.
— (2017) *American Originality: Essays on Poetry*. Farrar, Straus & Giroux.

Goddard, Harold. (1951) *The Meaning of Shakespeare*. University of Chicago Press.

Heaney, Seamus. (1998) *Opened Ground, Poems 1966–1996*. Faber & Faber.

— (2002) *Finders Keepers*. Faber & Faber.

— (1988) *The Government of the Tongue*. Faber & Faber.

Hirsch, Edward. (1999) *How to Read a Poem and Fall in Love with Poetry*. Harcourt.

Hogan, Caelainn. (2020) *Republic of Shame*. Penguin.

Holquist, M. (1990) *Dialogism: Bakhtin and his World*. Routledge.

Howe, P.P. (1928–32) *Complete Works of William Hazlitt*, 21 vols. J.M. Dent and Sons.

Jeffares, N. & Anthony, K. (eds) (1992) *Irish Childhoods*. Gill and Macmillan.

Joyce, James. (1916) *Portrait of the Artist as a Young Man*.

Keats, John. (1988) *The Complete Poems*. Penguin.

Lear, J. (1990) *Love and Its Place in Nature*. Faber & Faber.

Lieberman, J. (1993) *Acts of Will: The Life and Work of Otto Rank*. University of Massachusetts Press.

Linscott, R. (ed.) (1959) *Selected Poems and Letters of Emily Dickinson*. Anchor Books

Loewald, H. (1980) *Papers on Psychoanalysis*. Yale University Press.

— (1998) *Sublimation: Inquiries into Theoretical Psychoanalysis*. Yale University Press.

Lonergan, B. (1958) *Insight: A Study of Human Understanding*. Longmans.

McGahern, John. (1963) *The Barracks*. Faber & Faber.

— (1985) *High Ground*. Faber & Faber.

— (2002) *That They May Face the Rising Sun*. Faber & Faber.

— (2005) *Memoir*. Faber & Faber.

— (2009) *Love of the World*. Faber and & Faber.

Morgan, Charles. (1960) *The Writer and His World*. Macmillan.

Murry, John Middleton. (1925) *Keats and Shakespeare*. Oxford University Press.

Nagel, T. (1986) *The View from Nowhere*. Oxford University Press.
Newman, J.H. (1959) *The Idea of a University*. Image Books.
O'Driscoll, Dennis. (2008) *Stepping Stones: Interviews with Seamus Heaney*. Faber & Faber.
Oliver, Mary. (1998) *Rules of the Dance*. Mariner Books.
Proust, Marcel. (1983) *Remembrance of Things Past*. Penguin.
— (1988) *Days of Reading*. Penguin.
Resnik, S. (1987) *The Theatre of the Dream*. Tavistock.
Rovelli, Carlo. (2018) *The Order of Time*. Penguin.
Rudnytsky, P. (1991) *The Psychoanalytic Vocation*. Yale University Press.
Rycroft, C. (1958) *Imagination and Reality*. Hogarth.
— (1991) *Viewpoints*. Hogarth.
Sachs, H. (1951) *The Creative Unconscious*. Cambridge, MA: Sci-Art Publishers.
Salomon, E. (1976) English Translation of 'Dream and Poetry' by Otto Rank. *Journal of the Otto Rank Association*. Vol. 11. Number 1.
Sampson, Denis. (2014) *A Migrant Heart*. Linda Leith Publishing.
Scally, Derek. (2022) *The Best Catholics in the World*. Penguin.
Sharpe, E.F. (1937) *Dream Analysis*. Hogarth.
— (1950) *Collected Papers on Psychoanalysis*. London. Hogarth.
Simic, Charles. (2015) *The Life of Images*. Harper Collins.
Symington, Neville. (1993) *Emotion and Spirit*. Karnac.
— (2012) *The Psychology of the Person*. Karnac.
— (2018) *A Different Path*. Sphinx.
— The Personal Mystery of Being. Unpublished paper.
Vlastos, G. (1991) *Socrates: Ironist and Moral Philosopher*. Cambridge University Press.
Watson, Peter. (2000) *A Terrible Beauty*. Phoenix Press.
Whelan, Maurice. J. Ford, D. Mongon. (1982) *Special Education and Social Control*. RKP.
Whelan, Maurice (ed.) (2000) *Mistress of Her Own Thoughts: Ella Freeman Sharpe and the Practice of Psychoanalysis*. Rebus Press.
Whelan, Maurice (2004) *Thoughts for the Twenty-first Century: In the Company of William Hazlitt*. Australian Scholarly Publishing.

— (2008) *Boat People*. Ginninderra Press.
— (2009) *The Lilac Bow*. Ginninderra Press.
— (2011) *Excalibur's Return*. Ginninderra Press.
— (2014) *A Season and a Time*. Ginninderra Press.
— (2017) *Spirit Eye*. Ginninderra Press.
White, R.S. (1966) *Hazlitt as a Reader of Shakespeare*. Edwin Mellen Press.
— (1985) *Let Wonder Seem Familiar*. Humanities Press.
— (1987) *Keats as a Reader of Shakespeare*. Athlone Press.

Index

A

Allen, Christopher 179, 197
Altimira 151, 156, 167, 168
Ariel 31, 32, 33
Armstrong, Karen 150, 151, 152
Arnold, Matthew 227
Auden, W.H. 164, 193

B

Benedict XVI 49, 87, 105
Berlin, Isaiah 115, 117
Bloom, Harold 31, 176
Boat People 21, 22
Bohr, Niels 163
Borne, Ludwig 40
Brahmodya 152, 156, 172, 175, 179
Brown, George Mackay 25, 26
Brown, Michael 51, 74, 75
Bruno, Giordano 114, 116, 197
Burke, Edmund 96, 223, 227

C

Caliban 31, 235, 237
Catholic church 12, 17, 18, 46, 47, 48, 49, 50, 84, 87, 88, 89, 90, 92, 94, 99, 100, 101, 102, 103, 104, 106, 111, 114, 131, 144
Catholic emancipation 98, 127
clerical child sexual abuse 12, 18, 46, 47, 48, 49, 51, 52, 53, 55, 60, 61, 62, 63, 66, 67, 68, 72, 81, 83, 84, 86, 87, 88, 89, 91, 100, 106, 108, 112, 137, 183
clericalism 88, 99, 105, 131, 133
Clonliffe College 52, 56, 57, 70
Cloyne report 87
Coleridge, Mark 105, 106
Coleridge, Samuel Taylor 116, 121, 122, 130
Collins, Marie 60, 61, 62
Committee on Evil Literature 136, 138
Connell, Bishop 52, 53, 54, 61, 86
Costigan, Commissioner 51, 58
Covid-19 16
Crediting Poetry 29
Crimen sollicitationis 59, 87, 90, 100, 101
Crumlin hospital 58, 60
Cunnane, Archbishop 57

D

Darwin, Charles 38, 45, 101, 225
Dawkins, Richard 144, 146, 154
de Valera, Eamon 49, 51, 80, 136

Dei Filius 102
Descartes, René 163, 197
Dickinson, Emily 15, 18, 26, 107, 112, 120, 156, 172, 173, 176, 177, 186, 193, 210, 226, 234, 237
Dolan, Monsignor 54
Dragomir, Alexandru 236, 237
Dream Analysis 168
Dublin archdiocese 48, 52, 53, 60, 61
Dye, Daniel 88
Dyer, Edward 19, 205

E
Education of the Poet 16
Edwards, Ruth Dudley 78
Eichmann, Adolf 79, 80
Einstein, Albert 163, 170, 198
Evans, Arthur 163

F
Fairbairn, Ronald 67, 79, 81, 82, 124
Fawcett, Joseph 130, 131, 218, 223
Francis I 88, 90, 99, 105, 106, 129
Francis of Assisi, St 216
Freud, Sigmund 18, 35, 36, 37, 46, 79, 104, 124, 125, 135, 145, 146, 147, 148, 149, 164, 165, 166, 167, 168, 190, 209, 229, 230, 231

G
Garda/Gardaí 52, 86
Gedo, John 36
ghaoth 22, 23, 29, 47, 168, 204, 222

Gibran, Kahlil 158
Gleeson, Paddy 55
Glück, Louise 16, 207, 210, 241
Goddard, Harold 32
Granada Institute 53
Gray, Thomas 20
Griffin, Eddie 60

H
Haydon, Benjamin 107
Hazlitt, William 11, 18, 30, 40, 106, 107, 114, 116, 117, 118, 119, 120, 121, 122, 123, 124, 125, 126, 127, 128, 129, 130, 131, 132, 133, 153, 156, 173, 178, 205, 212, 216, 218, 223
Heaney, Seamus 23, 28, 29, 35, 122, 142, 156, 160, 188, 189, 190, 191, 192, 193
Heller, Hugo 38
Heraclitus 9, 15, 237
Higginson, Thomas 172, 173
Hirsch, Edward 19
Hughes, Ted 29

I
Idea of a University, The 98
Interpretation of Dreams, The 164, 166
Irish Privy Council 96

J
John Paul II 87
John XXIII 50, 87, 130
Joyce, James 13, 26, 136, 143, 206

K
Keats, John 30, 106, 107, 116,

122, 133, 156, 159, 174, 177, 214, 227
Kekule, August 162
Kenny, Enda 49, 66, 87, 88, 114, 135
King Lear 41, 211
Kinsella, Thomas 24
Kunitz, Stanley 234

L
Leo XIII 101
Lamentabili 101
Loewald, Hans 67, 68, 69, 70, 82, 83, 125, 149, 151, 157
Loewi, Otto 163
Lonergan, Bernard 13, 35, 86, 101

M
Macbeth 31, 38, 190
Malaquais, Jean 10, 185
Malouf, David 143
Manning, Cardinal 98
Martin, Diarmuid 52, 81, 85
Martin, L.C. 125
Maynooth College 76
McCarrick, Cardinal 89
McCellan, Peter 89
McGahern, John 10, 18, 26, 29, 33, 85, 98, 111, 135, 136, 137, 138, 139, 140, 141, 142, 143, 156, 176, 185, 188, 189, 206, 211, 224, 241
McGennis, Paul 58, 59, 60, 61, 142
McNamee, James 51
McQuaid, John Charles 51, 52, 56, 58, 59, 60, 80, 86, 137
Mendeleev, Dmitri 162

Moraru, Marin 235, 236, 237, 238
Morgan, Charles 157, 206
Mullarney, Janet 91
Murphy Commission 48, 52, 59, 61, 70, 81, 82

N
National Rehabilitation Hospital 53, 54, 55
Nicholson Museum 36
Nobel Prize 16, 147, 163, 207

O
O'Donohue, Maura 89
O'Driscoll, Denis 28, 142
O'Mahony, Bishop 54
Ogden, Thomas 169
On Transience 229, 230, 231
Osler, William 224, 225
Owen, Wilfred 111

P
Pascendi 101, 102, 103
Paul VI 87
Pearse, Patrick 74, 75, 76, 78, 79, 80
Pell, George 144
Penal Laws 95, 96
Persico, Bishop 88
Pfister, Oskar 145, 146, 147
Picasso, Pablo 163, 176
Pius XI 59, 70, 87, 90, 100
Planck, Max 163
Poems by Maurice Whelan
'Are We There Yet?' 159
'Cartography' 201
'Compass Line of Light, A' 212
'Dream's End' 171

'Engrafting New' 188
'Far Side of Time' 233
'Fringe Dweller' 93
'Gift of Writing, The' 207
'Hymn for Heaney' 192
'Introibo ad Altare Dei ' 92
'My Place on Earth' 242
'Of Birds and Poets' 239
'Old Ground' 202
'Perfect Pitch' 27
'Real Presence' 20
'What I Do' 228
'Your letter to the world arrived' 194
'Zero?' 160
Pontifical Secret 87, 90
Portrait of the Artist as a Young Man 13
Pound, Ezra 19
Prospero 26, 31, 32, 33
Proust, Marcel 35, 137, 143, 187, 192, 231, 232
psychoanalysis 13, 35, 36, 39, 44, 124, 145, 148, 149, 179, 210

R
Rank, Otto 165, 166
Redress of Poetry, The 23, 35
Reisinger (Wagner), Doris 89
Reynolds, Noel 52, 53, 54, 55, 56, 57, 70, 106, 142
Rilke, Maria Rainer 133, 204, 207
Rolland, Romain 147, 148, 149, 151
Ryan, Bishop 52, 56, 57, 86

S
Salamanca 29, 96, 168
Schnitzler, Arthur 38, 39, 135
Secreta Continere 87
Shakespeare, William 20, 30, 31, 32, 33, 38, 39, 41, 45, 112, 117, 118, 124, 134, 156, 159, 166, 167, 176, 180, 188, 190, 193, 226, 235, 238
Sharpe, Ella 11, 44, 125, 150, 167, 168, 179, 211
Simic, Charles 158
Socrates 45, 145
Sophie's Choice 68, 69
Spotlight 89
Stenson, Monsignor 53, 56, 61
Studies in Hysteria 35, 39
suicide 69, 70
Sycorax 31, 32
Sydney Institute for Psychoanalysis 36, 184, 186
Symington, Neville 148, 149, 158

T
talking cure 9
Tavistock Clinic 14, 63
Tempest, The 26, 30, 31, 212, 235, 238
Tennyson, Alfred Lord 186, 187, 204, 205
Tillich, Paul 144, 155
Trevaskis, Brian 51, 64, 74, 90, 135
Trinity College Dublin 49, 50, 51
Trump, Donald 112
Tyrrell, George 102, 103

W
Walsh, Patrick 53, 54
Watson, Peter 163
Whishaw, Ben 106, 107
Wordsworth, William 28, 123, 128

writing cure 10
Wuerl, Donald 88

X
Xiaobo, Liu 129, 238, 239

www.ingramcontent.com/pod-product-compliance
Lightning Source LLC
Chambersburg PA
CBHW030035100526
44590CB00011B/208